Praise for

Hunting the First State:
A Guide to Delaware Hunting

"I had a chance to enjoy your book and found that it brought back a lot of great memories of hunts long past."

- **John Sigler, Former President**
National Rifle Association

"Steven's work on *Hunting The First State* provides an amazing insight into the pursuit of your passions in Delaware. His research and effort into creating this valuable resource for hunters and his writing style brings in readers and motivates them to get out and hunt this great state."

- **Kevin Paulson, CEO**
HuntingLife.com

"Many of the same species of wild birds and animals that are found in the author's home state also are found here. The methods that work there should work here. Read and learn."

- **Dave Richey**
DaveRichey.com

"I could not think of a better writer than Steven M. Kendus, a lifelong resident of the First State and veteran hunter, to write this book. *Hunting the First State* represents the author's vast knowledge of the various game species and hunting opportunities this state has to offer to the avid outdoorsman."

- **Othmar Vohringer, Founder**
Smart Hunting Strategies - OthmarVohringer.com

HUNTING
THE FIRST STATE

A Guide to Delaware Hunting

Second Edition

Steven M. Kendus

Steven M. Kendus is a lifelong Delaware resident and avid outdoorsman dedicated to preserving hunting opportunities, lands, and traditions. He is a professional author, technical writer, and marketer, and has had various technical books and articles published. He is a member of multiple hunting, shooting, and conservation organizations, including the National Rifle Association, National Wild Turkey Federation, Ducks Unlimited, Safari Club International, Brandywine Hundred Rod and Gun Club, and Delaware State Sportmen's Association. Steven M. Kendus has a Bachelor of Arts in English – Business and Technical Writing from the University of Delaware and is a senior member of the Society for Technical Communication.

Printed in the United States of America by Lulu Press
(www.lulu.com)

To Lea, who excuses my field trips for six months of the year, and for Dominique and Gabriella, who are preserving the tradition.

Special thanks to hunting partners, mentors, and guides: Massey, Barkus, Bonanno, Quigley, and Morganstern.

Contents

WILD TURKEY HUNTING

Preface

Since the release of the first edition of *Hunting The First State: A Guide to Delaware Hunting* in 2007, I have received a great deal of feedback. Hunters and non-hunters alike have been pleasantly surprised with the depth of information presented in the book.

Humorously, some found it hard to believe that such a wealth of hunting opportunities exist in Delaware. While I was a guest on Cam & Company, a NRA news-based national radio show on Sirius XM's Patriot channel, host Cam Edwards joked that he thought topics related to Delaware hunting could be covered in a pamphlet rather than a book. I quickly cleared up that misconception by giving Cam and his audience a peak into the world of Delaware hunting.

I have received reviews, suggestions, comments, and photographs (some of which are featured in this book) from those who hunt Delaware and the surrounding region through www.HuntingTheFirstState.com, Facebook, and other means. This unsolicited feedback further proves the genuine interest in Delaware hunting facts, lore, tips, and tricks.

Hunting The First State serves multiple purposes. As a way to pass the time and build your overall knowledge about Delaware hunting, *Hunting The First State* can be read cover to cover. It is an enjoyable read that provides just the right mix of background information, statistics, personal stories, and photos. It is constructed in a logical, easy-to-follow fashion that enables you to smile, reflect, and learn at the same time.

Hunting The First State also serves as a reference guide that can be used over and over for researching specific topics related to Delaware hunting. Small enough to fit in your hunting pack, I even recommend taking a copy along with you on your hunts. It never hurts to quickly refresh your memory or to read about some tips and techniques that could increase your chances of success. Several hunters have told me they re-read the deer hunting chapter before the deer season begins, while others re-read the turkey hunting chapter while they are sitting in a pop-up blind waiting for a big gobbler to show up. Whatever your needs, *Hunting The First State* provides good reference material.

The very nature of this book lends itself to periodic updates. I encourage each of you to send me your feedback, suggestion, hunting stories, and photos. I frequently post stories and photos on www.HuntingTheFirstState.com and in my hunting column that I write for *The News Journal*. The Delaware hunting community is strong, so let's make sure our voices are heard.

Thanks for reading, and above all else, let's make sure we preserve the tradition.

Steven M. Kendus

1

About Delaware

Perfectly situated on the eastern seaboard between the Chesapeake Bay to the west and the Delaware River, Delaware Bay, and Atlantic Ocean to the east, Delaware has proven to be a hunting paradise for local sportsmen. For centuries, outdoorsmen and outdoorswomen have harvested the natural riches offered by the wild game that inhabit Delaware's deciduous forests, salt and freshwater marshes, and cultivated crop fields. Common game, such as white-tailed deer, Canada geese, and varied species of ducks have been targeted by the majority of Delaware hunters, but wild turkeys, woodcocks, quail, snow geese, crows, squirrels, and rabbits are also plentiful in Delaware and provide Delaware sportsmen with hours of hunting enjoyment each season.

While Delaware is the first state, it is also one of the smallest. Occupying a total area of 1,982 square miles, Delaware ranks 49th in the nation in size. With only three counties, New Castle, Kent, and Sussex, it is possible for a sportsman to enjoy a day's hunt that spans the entire state (since one can drive from the northernmost border of the state to the southernmost border in about two hours). Although Delaware ranks 49th in total area, it ranks approximately 45th in population according to the United States Census Bureau.

In 2000, Delaware's population was an estimated 783,600, and in 2009 the population was estimated to be 885,122.[1]

Of the 1,982 square miles, approximately ten percent of the land in Delaware is state-owned and open to public hunting. On public hunting lands, Delaware offers hunters State-owned deer stands and waterfowl blinds that are mostly issued by a governed lottery system. As a hunter who has hunted and harvested deer from State-owned deer stands, I can attest to the fact that "winning" the use of a stand through the lottery system is not difficult. Additionally, the State usually makes available any unclaimed stands or blinds on the mornings of scheduled hunts. Therefore, if a scheduled hunter does not claim his day's stand by a specified time, it is reissued via an onsite lottery.

While many Delaware public hunting lands offer deer stands and/or waterfowl blinds, additional hunting opportunities exist. Delaware game lands, including two national wildlife refuges, three state forests, ten state parks, and 17 wildlife management areas, offer various forms of hunting. Hunters should abide by all Delaware hunting laws and regulations as established in the annual *Delaware Hunting & Trapping Guide*, but they should also research and abide by any additional guidelines and regulations that may be established for individual public hunting locations. On the public hunting lands, hours can be spent walking the woods and hedgerows hunting squirrels, rabbits and quail; sitting motionless on the field edges hunting doves and crows; stomping the marshy bottoms in search of woodcocks and rails; and staking out the many marshes, ponds, streams, and

---

[1]U.S. Census Bureau, Population Finder - Delaware.

Scenes like this one, where deer habitat meets residential and agricultural land, are common in Delaware.

river edges in order to jumpshoot and passhoot geese and ducks.

According to the Delaware Division of Fish and Wildlife, 19,274 Delaware hunting licenses were issued in 2009[2] (16,677 resident licenses and 2,597 non-resident licenses), which means less than two percent of Delaware's residents hunt Delaware lands. If we consider that there are approximately 20,000 hunters in Delaware per year, and there are close to 40,000 resident deer[3] and vast numbers of migratory geese and ducks that use Delaware's fields and estuary systems as

---

[2] Delaware Division of Fish and Wildlife. *Delaware Hunting & Fishing License Statistics.*

[3] Rogerson, *Delaware Deer Management Plan 2010 – 2019 A Guide to How and Why Deer are Managed in The First State.*

stopping points on their annual migrations south, it only makes sense that Delaware is a hunting hotspot that has satisfied its resident sportsmen for years.

Aggressive deer management programs in Delaware have led to ever increasing numbers of deer, and the State's efforts, in conjunction with the U.S. Fish and Wildlife Service's guidelines and regulations, are leading to increases in waterfowl populations. With deer and geese plentiful in Delaware, many see the animals as nuisance species. As with many areas of the United States, urban development is encroaching on wild land, and backyard deer and goose sighting are becoming increasingly common. With ornamental shrubbery, vegetables gardens, and lawns becoming expensive meals for Delaware's wildlife, landowner complaints are on the rise. What's more, Delaware's deer use their opportunistic feeding patterns to target commercial crops, especially corn and soybeans. The losses incurred by Delaware farmers are so large, in fact, that in 2006 the Delaware Division of Fish and Wildlife began offering the Severe Deer Damage Assistance Program to assist farmers experiencing severe crop loss due to deer browsing. Under the program, farmers receive extra deer harvest permits and extended harvest seasons. The most compelling part of the plan to the average Delaware hunter is the mandate that at least one hunter who is not an immediate family member or farm employee must be allowed to hunt the farm enrolled in the program. This requirement provides Delaware hunters with more opportunities to hunt successfully.

If you are a landowner in Delaware, or if you have permission to hunt private land in Delaware, you are afforded a wealth of additional hunting opportunities. It doesn't take rocket science to do the math: If ten percent of the land in Delaware is public, than 90 percent of the land has to be private! Granted, not all (or even a high percentage) of that 90 percent can be legally hunted, but there is enough available private land that is exploited by Delaware sportsmen each year. In fact, if we just look at the 2008/2009 Delaware White-tailed Deer Harvest Summary numbers from the State of Delaware, 88 percent of deer (12,245) were harvested on private land[4]. Keep in mind that it is unlawful in Delaware to hunt on private land without the landowner's permission, so keep your ears open. Ask around. Talk to friends, neighbors, and fellow hunters. Don't be afraid to ask someone if you can hunt their property. It is only logical that some of the landowners and farmers who complain about "nuisance" wildlife will grant you permission to hunt their property. Additionally, some farmers and other owners of large land plots lease the hunting rights to their properties. If possible, locate and procure a hunting lease or join up with fellow hunters who are looking for an additional partner in their lease. Delaware also has several private clubs that exist to promote hunting and the shooting sports. In addition to hunting property, typically these clubs offer any combination of rifle ranges, pistol ranges, archery ranges, and skeet and trap ranges. Ask other hunters and shooters, research the World Wide Web, or ask the manager of your favorite hunting supply store for information on local hunting clubs.

Although only two percent of Delawareans are licensed hunters, hunting traditions are strong in the state. In most cases, hunting traditions are passed on through families,

---

[4] Delaware Division of Fish and Wildlife. *2008/09 Delaware White-tailed Deer Harvest Summary.*

where children learn hunting safety, etiquette, techniques, and locations from their parents, grandparents, or other family members. Adding to the allure of hunting the Delaware region, locally segregated families and friends share their traditional beliefs, legends, customs, and stories that make up the folklore and folklife of the Delaware hunting community. It is not uncommon to see a third-generation Delaware hunter deer hunting the same "secret spot" in the woods of Blackbird State Forest where his grandfather harvested a "220-pound, 12-point buck" 30 years prior. (Of course when the grandson asks for photos of the grandfather's deer, none exist because, in actuality, the deer was only a six-pointer the weighed 150 pounds!) Likewise, a shivering, wet, and enamored 7-year-old on his first goose hunt with his father and grandfather hears the stories of the "good ol' days when we were each allowed to shoot four geese per day for three months."[5] But he is soon brought back to reality when he is asked by his smiling father to use his numb fingers to hand-pick and clean the three Canadas they just shot.

Tagging along on his first hunt, gutting her first deer, picking his first goose, and sitting in her first deer stand are all traditions and rites of passage that are passed along through generations of Delaware hunters. Similarly, bragging rights, the best locations, the most effective camouflage, and the ability to embellish stories while discrediting those of hunting buddies are all traditions that are learned by listening to and imitating seasoned hunters. Unfortunately, these shared traditions and ways of life may be disappearing. Statistics indicate a steady decline in the number of licensed

---

[5] Delaware Division of Fish and Wildlife. *Canada goose management in Delaware.*

hunters in Delaware, which follows a nationwide trend. The chart on the following page illustrates the decline in the numbers of Delaware hunters over the past quarter century.

Competing pastimes, societal pressures, and diminished hunting lands are just some of the factors that seem to be contributing to decreased interest in hunting. With this steady decline in the number of licensed hunters, it is important to preserve the traditions associated with hunting the Delaware region. The subsequent chapters aim to preserve Delaware's hunting legacy by discussing important history, techniques, locations, tips, and tricks associated with Delaware hunting and by providing anecdotes that contribute to and support the associated folklore.

Delaware Hunting License Statistics

Hunting Licenses - Historical Summary[6]		
License Year	Number of Resident Hunting Licenses	Number of Non-Resident Hunting Licenses
1984	23,644	3,516
1985	24,269	3,728
1986	21,781	3,885
1987	23,378	4,320
1988	21,109	4,667
1989	21,411	4,192
1990	21,157	3,848
1991	21,674	2,995
1992	21,863	2,362
1993	21,664	2,184
1994	21,769	2,042
1995	19,518	1,945
1996	19,914	1,693
1997	20,257	1,731
1998	19,886	1,993
1999	19,422	2,295
2000	19,468	1,915
2001	18,921	1,997
2002	19,299	2,189
2003	18,088	2,017
2004	16,663	1,847
2005	16,957	2,599
2006	16,970	2,711
2007	17,013	2,877
2008	16,114	2,632
2009	16,677	2,597

---

[6] Delaware Division of Fish and Wildlife. Delaware Hunting & Fishing License Statistics.

2

White-tailed Deer Hunting

From Brandywine Creek State Park and the backyards of Greenville in New Castle County through Bombay Hook National Wildlife Refuge in Kent County and Redden State Forest and Assawoman Wildlife Area in Sussex County, Delaware sportsmen have traversed marshy bottoms, endured swarming mosquitoes, braved poison ivy vines as thick as broom handles, and laughed in the face of pelting ice storms to pursue Delaware's biggest hunting prize — the elusive white-tailed deer.

When most people think of hunting in the eastern United States, they think of the white-tailed deer (or just 'deer' to Delawareans) first. Many non-hunters have unrealistic and fantastic views of deer hunters as boorish, uneducated oafs who stomp through the woods each fall wearing red plaid jackets, carrying high-power rifles, and toting six-packs of Budweiser. Add to that visual the stereotypical beard, missing teeth, and Elmer Fudd-style hat, and you begin to get the picture. To many, we hunters are the guys who killed Bambi's mom, caused the decline of bald eagles, and placed every piece of litter in the woods. We hunters know otherwise.

I would love to refute all of the stereotypes mentioned in the previous paragraph, but I can't! I won't! After all, I love my plaid wool hunting coats so much that I frequently find myself searching eBay for more vintage-style hunting garb! And let's face it: keeping a beard is much easier than shaving every morning. What's more, to a guy like me, those Elmer Fudd-style hats are pretty cool! They must appeal to someone other than me, or well-known retailers like Filson and Stormy Kromer wouldn't sell them! However, some of those deer hunter stereotypes couldn't be farther from the truth. It takes patience, skill, knowledge, and practice to harvest a deer, and most of us put hours, days, and even weeks of research into our sport. We read books and articles, visit web sites, watch videos, physically scout deer habitat, and actually observe deer to make ourselves better, more effective, and more ethical hunters. As proponents of fair chase principles and firearms safety, we don't mix alcohol with guns. We don't fire indiscriminately at targets, be they alive or not. And we have no interest in polluting or otherwise harming the natural resources that we love. (Plus, to further disprove the negative stereotypes, hunters are not even allowed to hunt deer with high-power rifles in Delaware!)

The passion that lives within each deer hunter is in a class by itself and is difficult to describe to a non-hunter. Curt Barkus, a lifelong New Castle, Delaware resident and avid hunter, sums it up best in a way that only he can pull off. "There is no comparison to the time spent in the great outdoors. I love having the opportunity to harvest a deer, but more than that, I just love being close to nature. Whether I see

Delaware hunter Curt Barkus, a stealthy, self-taught archer and master of camouflage, concealment, and deer stalking, consistently harvests some of the biggest bucks in Delaware.

a deer on a hunt or not, I enjoy watching the birds, squirrels, rabbits, and whatever else I come across. Plus, there is no rush that compares to the rush of a close encounter with a white-tail."

Now I have crossed paths with a multitude of Delaware hunters, trappers, and fisherman since the 1980s, but I have encountered no character as intriguing, engaging, knowledgeable (and yes, eccentric) as Curt Barkus. Picture a fairy tale science project gone awry in which Santa Claus is crossed with Sasquatch. Now upload the Hunting and Fishing sections of your local bookstore into his brain, and you end up with Curt Barkus.

Sporting his mottled, black, white, and gray beard (that he swears makes him more camouflaged), hauling a ready-to-rupture, 60-plus-pound pack on his pack (with everything from Jolly Ranchers and sardines to saws and spare flashlights in it), and carrying his Black Widow recurve bow, Curt is a site to be seen – *or unseen*. As a traditional archer, Curt is a stealthy, self-taught archer and master of camouflage, concealment, and deer stalking who consistently harvests some of the biggest bucks in Delaware. Through my own experiences and with the close mentoring of guys like Barkus and hunting supply store owner and hunting guide John Massey, I have compiled the following techniques, locations, tips, and tricks to assist you with your Delaware deer hunting.

Delaware Deer Habitat

Most of Delaware is situated on the Atlantic coastal plain, although northern New Castle County sits on the Piedmont plateau, a hilly area extending from parts of Alabama through parts of New Jersey that separates the Appalachian Mountains and the Atlantic coastal plain. Much of the land in

Delaware is at or near sea level, so acclimating your lungs to the elevation is not a problem. After all, the highest point in Delaware is a mere 447 feet above sea level. Likewise, Delaware's climate is not one of extremes, with average monthly temperatures ranging from about 75 degrees Fahrenheit in summer to about 32 degrees Fahrenheit in fall. Granted, summertime high temperatures frequently extend into the 90s (and rarely into the 100s), and wintertime temperatures sometimes dip into the teens and single digits, but there are few days that are truly unbearable to Delaware sportsmen. (Keep in mind, however, that if you plan to participate in archery deer seasons that typically begin in September, be prepared to hunt in hot and humid conditions. Likewise, if you plan to participate in late season January and February hunts, you very well could experience sub-freezing temperatures, ice, and snow.) The moderate Delaware temperatures provide for productive growing seasons, and the combination of ample food supplies and relatively mild winters directly support Delaware's deer population.

As with most white-tailed deer throughout North America, Delaware's deer graze on tree leaves, grasses, broadleaved herbs, backyard vegetables, farmers' crops, and wild fruits and berries in spring and summer, and acorns, nuts, twigs, tree bark, and available grasses in the fall and winter. The abundance of available, high-quality food throughout Delaware makes it easy to see why many Delaware deer hunters are successful each season. With Delaware whitetails feeding on nutrient-rich wild acorns, chestnuts, and hickory nuts and on cultivated corn, soybeans, and wheat, it is not uncommon for hunters to encounter and harvest big, mature bucks with trophy-quality racks.

Paul Quigley with a mature doe taken by bow in late fall.

Likewise, with Delaware's increased efforts in overall deer herd management, harvesting of mature does is encouraged. In fact, hunters who are just as concerned with deer management and venison steaks as they are with wall-hanging bruiser bucks frequently harvest multiple does per year. According to Delaware's 2008/09 White-tailed Deer Harvest Summary, 45% percent of the deer harvested (6238) were adult does, and 10.2% (1409) were fawn does.[7] While many older hunters still stick to the old belief that it is the equivalent of sacrilege to harvest does, the State of Delaware has done an adequate job in educating most hunters about the benefits of harvesting does.

---

[7] *2008/09 Delaware White-tailed Deer Harvest Summary.*

Note: In 2010, Delaware's Division of Fish & Wildlife took deer management planning, practice, and education to a new level by issuing their 102-page *Delaware Deer Management Plan*. The plan, created with input from a public phone survey, a mail survey to hunters, and a 22-member advisory group made up of a diverse representation of Delaware hunters and non-hunters alike, outlines goals and strategies for managing deer populations, habitat, damage, recreation, education, and resources for 2010 through 2019. It appears to be a tremendous first step in establishing sensible and effective deer management strategies.

Delaware's terrain is quite diverse, but the adaptive whitetails can be found in just about every area of the state. From state parks, wood lots, and backyards to corn fields, state forests and fresh- and saltwater marshes, Delaware's deer can be found in surprisingly high concentrations. To have your best chances of success when hunting Delaware deer, conduct some preliminary research into the areas you are considering hunting. Scout out nearby food and water sources, types of cover, and natural funnels or high-traffic areas that are created by terrain features, such as where a heavy wood narrows to a finger and protrudes into a corn field. Also talk with other hunters who have hunted a specific location or locations with similar types of features because the best hunting times, techniques, and attire will differ based upon the type of terrain you are hunting. The Internet is also proving to be a tremendous tool for assisting with Delaware deer hunting due diligence. With new satellite mapping and aerial photo utilities (such as Google Earth) and the availability of Delaware public hunting area maps online, hunters are frequently using Internet resources to plan their hunts.

Deer Hunting Methods

If you are accustomed to hunting deer in the mountains of Pennsylvania, or if you revel in taking long rifle shots at game in the open expenses of the American West, you will be in for quite a surprise when you hunt Delaware deer. Because of Delaware's flat elevation, relatively small hunting areas, and concentrated population, Delaware hunters are limited in the methods in which they may hunt deer. Rifles cannot be used to hunt deer in Delaware, but as of the 2009-2010 hunting season, separate seasons exist for archery (both vertical bows and crossbows), shotgun, muzzleloader, and handgun.

Archery and Crossbow

As a deer hunter who hunts with a compound bow about 90% of the time, I cannot make this any clearer: *If you want more opportunities to harvest Delaware deer, be they trophy-quality bucks or freezer-filling does, hunt with a bow.* The 2008/2009 Delaware White-tailed Deer Harvest Summary reports that about 12% of the deer were harvested with bows[8], which, at first, seems to contradict my statement. However, I specifically referenced "more *opportunities* to harvest Delaware Deer." Consider this: As of the 2009-2010 hunting season, a deer hunter who participates in the Delaware archery season can legally hunt deer Monday through Saturday September 1 through January 31. That means a Delaware bowhunter can legally hunt about 125 days a year! When compared with the 60 or so days per year where Delaware hunters can use firearms to hunt deer (assuming they hunt every day of each of the muzzleloader, shotgun,

---

[8] *2008/09 Delaware White-tailed Deer Harvest Summary.*

Traditional archer Curt Barkus harvests a Delaware fall buck on public land.

and handgun seasons), it is easy to see the additional number of opportunities afforded to Delaware bowhunters.

In addition to the increased number of hunting opportunities, Delaware bowhunters also boost their chances of harvesting deer for several other reasons. First, there are fewer hunters in the woods. With fewer hunters walking into and out of deer stands, driving all-terrain vehicles through deer bedding areas, and parking cars and slamming doors at the edges of deer feeding areas, deer are less likely to be spooked and will be more likely to stick to their daily patterns. With the first Delaware deer firearms season usually not taking place until early- to mid-October, Delaware bowhunters have the woods to themselves for at least a month. Second, late summer and early fall foliage and standing crops not only provide easily discernable food sources for deer, they also provide phenomenal camouflage. With many of the whitetails' favorite food sources still plentiful in late summer and early fall, a bowhunter can maximize his odds by hunting established trails and funnels that lead to existing food plots. Likewise, a bowhunter can increase his chances of harvesting a Delaware deer because the above average camouflage he needs to draw a bow without being seen is readily available. Full trees with green leaves, tall green corn stalks, thick hedgerows, and even stands of phragmites make excellent camouflage.

While many bowhunters typically want to hunt from tree stands, seasoned archers will tell you that hunting from the ground in the late summer and early fall is just as effective because of the lush and diverse flora. Traditional archer Curt Barkus routinely hunts from the ground. "Why bowhunt from a tree?" asks Barkus. "I have killed way more deer from the ground. In a tree, you are limited to what walks within 35 yards of your stand. If you are on the ground, you can use your camouflage and your mobility to your advantage. Rather than waiting for the deer to walk by my tree stand, I can move to them."

Owner of Shooters Supply in New Castle, Delaware, John Massey is a skilled bowhunter and bow technician.

As of 2009-2010, Delaware bowhunters may use compound bows, recurve bows, long bows, or crossbows during the Delaware archery and crossbow deer seasons.[9] The

---

[9] *Delaware Hunting & Trapping Guide*, 18.

decision to use a crossbow or a compound, recurve, or long bow to hunt Delaware deer is strictly determined by each hunter's preference, and arguments can be made for and against each type of bow. Bowhunters' preferences and skill levels evolve over time, and their choices in bow types may change as well. I have seen natural born archers who can essentially pick up any bow and be deadly accurate within taking two or three shots, and I have seen other bowhunters who struggle with their shooting. Whichever the case, all bowhunters must practice so that they are confident in their equipment and their shooting technique.

During Delaware archery and crossbow deer seasons, most public hunting areas are open for hunting. Many areas have special bow hunting regulations regarding public deer stand use, private deer stand use, deer that are allowed to be harvested, parking, and sign-in/sign-out procedures, so be sure to research the areas in which you will hunt. Additionally, bowhunters may hunt with bows (vertical and crossbows) during any Delaware firearms season as long as they wear at least 400 square inches of visible hunter orange on their chests, backs, and heads.[10]

Shotgun

With 67% (9,219) of the deer harvested in Delaware during the 2008-2009 season taken by shotgun[11], it is plain to see that shotgun is the traditional harvest method of choice by the majority of Delaware hunters. In fact, many Delaware hunters rigidly define their hunting seasons as the two incomparable weeks of the year when they can hunt bucks

---

[10] *Delaware Hunting & Trapping Guide*, 18.

[11] *2008/09 Delaware White-tailed Deer Harvest Summary.*

with shotguns. Like other areas of the country where white-tailed deer hunting monopolizes the minds of sportsmen throughout the fall and winter, many Delaware hunters take vacations (or sick time) from their jobs and forsake all that is dear to them (including their families, non-hunting friends, and even the Philadelphia Eagles) to focus solely on deer hunting. As an avid Eagles fan who attends most home games and watches just about every away game on television, Sunday football games present no conflicts. However, I distinctly recall trying to listen to an Eagles Saturday playoff game while deer hunting. I was in a tree stand in a driving sleet storm trying to hear static-filled play-by-play through a junky, old transistor radio! As you can see, hunting takes precedence.

Each fall, deer hunters begin their preparations by scouting their favorite hunting grounds, dusting off years old camouflage clothes and faded orange vests, and sniffing all the new deer scent attractants to determine exactly which mysterious liquid smells the most like a doe that is hotter than the mid-day August sand on Dewey Beach. They spend hours 'BS-ing' with proprietors, employees, and customers at their local hunting supply store. They talk about big bucks they've seen throughout the summer and fall (though they are careful not to divulge the locations of their sightings). And they head to the shooting ranges to once again sight in the shotguns that they've had since they were really too young to hold them steady.

Every hunter, female or male, young or old, prepares for the shotgun season with similar hopes. They hope they won't sit for hours on end in a deer stand seeing and hearing nothing more than scurrying gray squirrels, chattering blue jays, and the occasional slink of a red fox. They hope they will get the big, bruising wall-hanger, the associated glory, and the years of stories that go with it. And, most of all, they hope they at least get a shot at harvesting something for the freezer.

John Massey, owner of Shooter's Supply, a well-known hunting, fishing, and shooting supply store on Route 13 in New Castle, Delaware that has served the needs of Delaware hunters since 1964, witnesses firsthand the annual preparation of Delaware shotgun hunters. "It usually begins in late summer with some guys checking out the latest equipment and bore sighting their guns. Store traffic picks up in September, but then it gets hot and heavy during October and November. We sell a ton of shotguns, shells, deer scents, and hunter's orange right up to the last day of the fall shotgun season," explains Massey. "I see the same faces year and after year, I hear the same stories, and I can even predict who will show up at the last minute. It's my favorite time of the year."

Typically, Delaware establishes two seven- or eight-day long shotgun seasons in which hunters can harvest bucks or does. The first season occurs in November and traditionally coincides with the 'rut,' the time when bucks are most active in searching for does to breed. This season is viewed by almost all hunters as the best time to get a chance at harvesting a mature, trophy buck, since a buck's hormones tend to skew his normally super-keen sense of self-preservation. During November, Delaware deer tend to be in smaller clusters or family groups, with mature bucks being somewhat solitary. Many of the whitetails' main food sources are still available, and an experienced hunter can predict with some degree of accuracy the best hunting locations. Many trees have multi-colored or brown leaves, and some green still exists throughout the woods. The multiple colors and

Author Steven Kendus poses with a post-rut, 6-point Delaware buck taken in January.

textures provide adequate camouflage for the hunter and the deer.

The second shotgun season usually occurs in January, when the temperatures are much colder, deer food supplies are less plentiful, and available cover and camouflage are greatly diminished. With the rut over, Delaware whitetails tend to congregate in much bigger herds (of males and females) during the winter months. The seasoned Delaware hunter knows that hunting location is key at this time of year. Individual deer may not be as dispersed as they were in November, but if a hunter is at the right spot at the right time, he can have a herd of 30 deer or more pass within shotgun range. Ample opportunities exist for harvesting bucks and does, but hunters should be aware that some bucks could have dropped their antlers by this time.

In recent years, Delaware has implemented special antlerless only shotgun deer seasons, in which hunters may only harvest antlerless deer or deer with both antlers less than three inches long. Implementing these antlerless, or 'doe seasons' as many Delaware hunters call them, has helped the State of Delaware properly manage the overall Delaware deer herd. As mentioned early, many hunters have traditionally despised the notion of harvesting any does, but Delaware's education efforts and antlerless seasons are working to change these beliefs. According to the Quality Deer Management Association:

> Quality Deer Management (QDM) is a management philosophy/practice that unites landowners, hunters, and managers in a common goal of producing biologically and socially balanced deer herds within existing environmental, social, and legal constraints. This approach typically involves the protection of young bucks (yearlings and some 2.5 year-olds) combined with an adequate harvest of female deer to maintain a healthy population in balance with existing habitat conditions and landowner desires. This level of deer management involves the production of quality deer (bucks, does, and fawns), quality habitat, quality hunting experiences, and, most importantly, quality hunters.[12]

With this increased emphasis on managing Delaware's deer herd, many more hunters are given the opportunity to harvest a Delaware deer. To beginning hunters, hunters with limited time, and hunters whose mouths water at the mention

---

[12] Quality Deer Management Association. *What is Quality Deer Management?*.

of venison steaks on the grill, harvesting does is a welcome mission.

Keep in mind that while there are few hunters in the woods during the Delaware archery season, the exact opposite is true for the Delaware shotgun seasons. With so many hunters anxiously awaiting the Delaware shotgun seasons each year (especially the season during the November rut), they make it their duties to hunt as much as they possibly can during the week-long season. The increase in the number of hunters leads to increased hunting pressure, which can affect where you hunt, when you hunt, and how you hunt. When hunting public locations, be aware that most of the public stands are probably filled with other hunters. Because of the increased human presence in the woods, deer may change their habits and patterns, and subsequently your pre-season scouting conclusions may not hold true. However, you can use the increased number of hunters to your benefit. The sight, sound, and smell of humans can cause deer to move. Arrive at your hunting location and get settled in before the other hunters, doing everything possible to be quiet and unseen. As other hunters begin to move to their locations, they may cause deer to move toward you. Likewise, listen for gun shots near your location, since the sound of the shots could cause startled deer to move toward you. If you are hunting private land, try your best not to spook any deer, especially if you have public hunting areas nearby. Speaking from experience, it is not uncommon to leave a public hunting area after a day of seeing few deer only to see an entire herd standing in the open of an adjacent private field. Deer know to move away from hunting pressure, and they frequently find much less pressure on private land. During the shotgun seasons in Delaware, try your best to use the hunting pressure to your advantage.

According to typical Delaware regulations, Delaware shotgun deer hunters can use shotguns no smaller than 20 gauge and can use slugs, pumpkin ball, or buckshot loads to harvest deer. All shotguns with a magazine, regardless of gauge, must be plugged to hold only three shells in the chamber and magazine combined. Additionally, it is illegal to carry shot smaller than buckshot while deer hunting.

Most Delaware deer hunters tend to use 12-gauge shotguns with slugs for longer distance shooting (up to 125 yards) or with buckshot for closer, faster-moving targets. For additional power and range, some hunters use 10-gauge shotguns, while other hunters choose shoulder-saving 20-gauges. To many, the make and model of the gun are unimportant, though just about everyone has their favorite. The common Remingtons, Winchesters, and Mossbergs are prevalent, but pretty much every shotgun manufacturer is represented in the Delaware deer woods and fields. Traditional pump-action guns are used, as are semi-automatic shotguns, single-shot shotguns, over-unders, and side-by-sides. To achieve the best accuracy, many experts recommend using shotguns specially designed with rifled barrels for shooting slugs. When I hunt deer with a shotgun, I typically use the Remington Model 870 Express Slug gun, which is designed with a rifled barrel and cantilever scope mount. As with all Delaware hunting regulations, consult the annual *Delaware Hunting & Trapping Guide* for detailed regulations.

Muzzleloader

For hunters looking for an added, more traditional challenge when deer hunting, Delaware typically offers two muzzleloader deer seasons. Usually held in early- to mid-October and mid- to late-January, the muzzleloader (or "black powder") seasons offer hunters additional opportunities to harvest Delaware deer. (It is important to note that Delaware regulations have traditionally allowed hunters to hunt with a muzzleloader during shotgun deer seasons, as well.)

Although hunting with a muzzleloader has become much easier in recent years, the fact remains that muzzleloaders present interesting challenges to hunters. Essentially, muzzleloading firearms require that a shooter loads the gun by inserting gunpowder (or a similar propellant) into the gun barrel (muzzle), then using a ramrod to firmly seat a projectile (slug or ball) against the powder and ram both to the base (or breech) of the barrel. The method in which the gunpowder is ignited depends on the type of muzzleloader used.

Primitive muzzleloaders, such as the rifles used by American explorers and folk heroes Daniel Boone and Davy Crockett, use complicated ignition systems. Flintlock firearms require that the hammer hold a piece of flint that causes a spark when the hammer strikes a metal plate. In turn, the spark ignites a small portion of black powder held in a small pan. The ignited powder in the pan then ignites the remaining powder in the breech, causing the projectile to shoot out of the barrel. Similarly, though somewhat easier to use, caplock or percussion muzzleloaders ignite the gunpowder in the breech by using a percussion cap and a small nipple to force a flame into the breech. The hammer strikes the cap, causing a spark that moves through the nipple and into the breech, thereby igniting the powder and firing the projectile.

If you want to recreate the hunting experience of your forefathers, hunting with a primitive muzzleloader is the way to do it. However, be aware that flintlock muzzleloaders may not fire immediately after squeezing the trigger. In some cases, a one- to two-second delay may occur prior to the powder igniting. Also, foul weather may hamper the flintlock's ability to function properly, since wet powder or flint can prevent the gun from firing. Caplock muzzleloaders are more reliable in foul weather, however, since their percussion caps can fire in any weather.

For Delaware deer hunters looking for an easier, more modern approach to muzzleloading, they should consider using inline muzzleloading technology. While the guns are loaded from the muzzle like primitive muzzleloader, inline muzzleloaders rely on a much simpler ignition system. In most inline muzzleloading systems, a shotgun primer or similar ignition disk is seated at the base of the breech, directly behind the powder. When the trigger is squeezed, much like a modern rifle, the hammer strikes the primer or disk and directly ignites the powder, causing the projectile to fire. The primers or disks are protected from the weather and will usually fire under the harshest of conditions. Additionally, pre-measured quantities of powder can be purchased in pellet form and are much easier to load than loose grains. When the powder pellets are coupled with modern saboted and jacketed bullets, loading (and reloading) time is drastically reduced, accuracy is enhanced, and barrel fouling is minimized because of cleaner burning powder.

Since primitive and inline muzzleloaders are used effectively to hunt deer in Delaware, the choice of which type to use is a personal one. Some traditionalists argue that inline muzzleloaders don't reflect the true spirit, difficulty, and character of the old "smokepoles" and essentially view inline muzzleloaders as glorified, single-shot rifles. Other hunters view inline muzzleloaders as more advanced, more effective, and therefore more ethical tools for harvesting deer, since their effective ranges can be up to 200 yards due to enhanced barrel rifling, propellants, and ignition systems. Both sides of the argument have valid points, though I have to say I have effectively used an inline .50-caliber Thomson Center Encore since 2002, and I love it. Besides practicing at the rifle range, I have fired it nine times and have killed nine deer, with the farthest shot being 107 yards. The 107-yard shot doesn't sound too impressive until you consider the facts that one, I was in a January snowstorm of heavy, wet snow; and two, I was able to reload quickly enough to fire a second shot and harvest a second deer. (Something tells me that I wouldn't have been able to do either with a flintlock!)

Although hunting with a muzzleloader is more difficult, many Delaware deer hunters actually prefer hunting with a muzzleloading firearm over a shotgun. The first muzzleloader season in Delaware traditionally takes place in October, before any shotgun season where bucks can be harvested. Therefore, many hunters in search of a wall-hanger believe the initial, pre-rut muzzleloader season is the best time to harvest a mature buck. In fact, the 2008/2009 Delaware White-tailed Deer Harvest Summary numbers show that 15.5% (2165) of the deer harvested were taken during the October and January muzzleloader seasons, second only to the number of deer harvested during the

November shotgun season.[13] With relatively low numbers of hunters in the woods and deer having little exposure to the sound of gunshots, chances of harvesting a deer by muzzleloader in October are pretty good.

For hunters who wish to employ more traditional or primitive skills in their hunts by using muzzleloaders, practice cannot be overemphasized. While the same is true with any firearm, it is especially important for hunters to familiarize themselves with their muzzleloaders prior to actually hunting. With sophisticated loading, ignition, cleaning, and lubricating, muzzleloaders require much more attention than traditional shotguns or rifles. Hunters should be sure to thoroughly read the owner's manual of the gun as well as any applicable laws that pertain specifically to muzzleloading firearms. In some states, it is legal to carry a muzzleloader in a vehicle that has powder and a bullet loaded in the barrel, as long as no ignition system (i.e. primer) is present; and in other states this practice is illegal. Also, muzzleloader hunters should be sure to practice shooting targets at different distances using different measures of powder, since ballistics will change with changes to propellant.

Handgun

Hunting deer with a handgun in Delaware is relatively new. Signed in to law in May 2005, the inaugural deer handgun season took place in January 2006. One hundred fourteen deer were harvested by handgun during the 2005-2006 hunting season[14], 135 during the 2006-2007 season[15], 163

---

[13] *2008/09 Delaware White-tailed Deer Harvest Summary.*

[14] *2005-06 Delaware White-tailed Deer Harvest Summary.*

during the 2007-2008 season, and 149 during the 2008-2009 season.[16]

Scheduled for early January, the Delaware handgun deer seasons provide late season hunters with additional, yet restricted, opportunities for harvesting deer. According to the 2010-2011 *Delaware Hunting & Trapping Guide*:

> Legal handguns are limited to revolvers and single shot pistols with a minimum barrel length of 5.75 inches and a maximum length of 12.5 inches and chambered for and using straightwall handgun ammunition in .357, .41 caliber, .41 magnum, .44 caliber, .44 magnum, .45 caliber, .454 caliber, .480 caliber or .50 caliber and using open sights, metallic/mechanical, optical or telescopic sights. Since the .460 casull is a .45 caliber, it is legal under the existing handgun legislation.[17]

Handguns must be openly carried on a sling or in a holster and cannot be concealed. Additionally, handgun hunting is only allowed on private land south of the Chesapeake and Delaware Canal (which crosses southern New Castle County, connecting the Delaware River and the Chesapeake Bay) and on designated state wildlife areas.

Hunters looking for an additional challenge and/or another week to harvest deer, have seemingly embraced the weeklong handgun season. In fact, according to the 2010-2011 *Delaware Hunting & Trapping Guide*, it is legal to hunt deer with a handgun at any time that a shotgun can legally be used. The handgun must be used in place of a shotgun. Hunters cannot carry both in the field at the same time.

---

[15] *2006/07 Delaware White-tailed Deer Harvest Summary.*

[16] *2007/08 and 2008/09 Delaware White-tailed Deer Harvest Comparison*

[17] *2010-2011 Delaware Hunting & Trapping Guide*, 23.

Deer Hunting Hotspots

Before committing my research and experiences about hot locations for hunting Delaware deer to paper, I questioned my sanity. Am I crazy for divulging Delaware deer hunting hotspots to the masses? Will my hunting partners black-list me for disclosing long-held deer hunting secrets? What if numerous readers hunt the locations I mention and no one harvests anything? With these questions in my mind, I decided it would be more beneficial to mention general areas that are traditional deer harvest hotspots instead of mentioning specific locations. Therefore, rather than mentioning a specific deer stand twenty paces east of an old oak tree, for example, I will discuss types of habitat that frequently hold lots of Delaware deer, and I will list general hunting areas (public and private) where quality deer are traditionally harvested.

Public Deer Stands Lotteries

As with other areas of the country, Delaware's best public deer hunting spots are at a premium. Until the 2010-2011 hunting season, an application for entering into Delaware's general public deer stand lottery was included in Delaware's annual *Delaware Hunting & Trapping Guide* (usually available online and from local sporting goods stores beginning in July). The general lottery application gave Delaware firearm hunters opportunities to procure good public hunting locations throughout the state. Hunters who wished to participate in the lottery were instructed to provide up to three dates and three public areas on which they wanted to hunt. Hunters also had the options to indicate if they were

A 2006 photo taken by Delaware hunter John Koval shows a doe and a piebald fawn on private, commercial property in New Castle County.

willing to accept dates or areas other than those requested on the form.

If hunters were selected in the lottery drawing, they were notified of their selected public stand location and were instructed to follow applicable check-in and check-out rules on the days of their hunts. However, if hunters were not selected in the pre-season lottery drawing, they could show up at designated public hunting check-in areas on hunting days and enter into drawings for any unclaimed public stands.

While some public stand locations were frequently requested by hunters on the pre-season lottery forms, there were usually unclaimed stands available at many public hunting areas on various days of the firearm deer hunting seasons. Therefore, the Delaware Division of Fish and Wildlife discontinued the general pre-season lottery in 2010. Instead, public deer stands will be awarded during on-site lotteries on the mornings of the hunts.

Public areas traditionally sought after in high volumes by hunters include Brandywine Creek State Park and Cedar Swamp Wildlife Management Area in New Castle County and Blackbird State Forest located on the border of New Castle and Kent Counties.

Although the public deer stand lottery is an excellent way to obtain a good *gun* hunting spot on public land, be aware that many public hunting areas in Delaware have different rules that apply to bowhunters. In many cases, bowhunters can hunt Delaware public hunting areas during archery-only seasons without prior reservations or lottery drawings. Be sure to thoroughly research the individual sets of rules and regulations for any public area you intend to hunt.

It is important to note that some public hunting areas in Delaware, including wildlife management areas, state parks, and national wildlife refuges, establish individual lottery systems and associated rules. Bombay Hook National Wildlife Refuge in Kent County, for example, is a deer hunting hotspot that establishes its own deer hunting lottery and regulations.

As of the 2010-2011 hunting season, a $20 Public Lands Blind Site permit is required to use public deer stands assigned through a lottery on Delaware state wildlife areas. Hunters must be in possession of the permit when using the stand.[18]

---

[18] *2010-2011 Delaware Hunting & Trapping Guide*, 43.

Hot Deer Management Zones

A few minutes of research goes along way. As with preparation for any hunt, you should spend some time researching any available information about the locales you wish to hunt. Before choosing a hunting location in Delaware, consider the deer harvest statistics and let them help you make an educated guess.

The Delaware Division of Fish and Wildlife divides Delaware into seventeen deer management zones, which are typically depicted on a map in the annual *Delaware Hunting & Trapping Guide*. According to the *2008/09 Delaware White-tailed Deer Harvest Summary*[19], the top three deer management zones for harvesting deer are Zone 11 in Sussex County, with 1,356 deer harvested; Zone 1 in northern New Castle County, with 1,231 deer harvested; and Zone 7 primarily in southwestern Kent County, with 1,146 deer harvested.

The table on page 36 illustrates the number of deer harvested in each management zone during the 2008-2009 hunting season. Granted, many of the deer harvested were taken on private land, but some public hunting areas exist within the top three Delaware deer management zones. Public hunting locations in Zone 11 include Redden State Forest, Old Furnace Wildlife Area, and the Industrial Forest Lands. Hot public hunting areas within Zone 1 include Brandywine Creek State Park, White Clay Creek State Park, the C&D Canal Wildlife Area, and Lums Pond State Park. (In fact, if rumor serves true, two of the biggest bucks harvested in Delaware in recent memory were taken in 2006 and 2010 at or near Lums Pond State Park.) Productive public hunting

---

[19] *2008/09 Delaware White-tailed Deer Harvest Summary.*

areas in Zone 16 include Trap Pond State Park and the Industrial Forest Lands.

Number of Deer Harvested in Each Management Zone (2008-2009)[20]

Deer Management Zone	Number of Deer Harvested
1	1,231
2	597
3	599
4	457
5	558
6	826
7	1,146
8	620
9	831
10	486
11	1,356
12	793
13	550
14	724
15	766
16	1,120
17	412

---

[20] *2008/09 Delaware White-tailed Deer Harvest Summary*

Overlooked Hotspots

If you want to beat the crowds and increase your chances of harvesting a monster Delaware buck, you have to hunt off the beaten path. Any hunter with a license and a gun can hunt the traditional, run-of-the-mill deer hunting locations like hardwood forests and agricultural fields, but it takes a special kind of hunter to seek out those special areas where deer experience less pressure. To pursue the deer that no other hunters are chasing, you must think outside the box. You must prepare yourself for longer walks to your hunting stand, the incessant hums of millions of mosquitoes, curious stares from homeowners, and the chance of getting soggy feet from rising tides.

Marshes along the Delaware River or Delaware Bay

With Delaware's entire eastern boundary bordered by water (the Delaware River, Delaware Bay, and Atlantic Ocean), saltwater and freshwater marshes are plentiful. With many of the marshes adjoined by farmland or woods, that natural flora of the marshes become an extension of the whitetails' habitat, and in turn, become attractive hunting locations.

Stands of phragmites that stretch for acres in all directions provide optimal cover and bedding for Delaware deer. There is no sight more descriptive of Delaware marsh hunting than a ten-point buck walking out of a marsh with caked-on mud up to his chest and stalks of phragmites lodged in his antlers. To hunters who target the marshes of the Delaware River, this sight is a common one.

Bill Poore with an 8-point backyard buck taken near New Castle County marshland.

Both the Augustine Wildlife Area and the C&D Canal Wildlife Area in New Castle County include hunting areas embedded in marshlands that border the Delaware River, and scores of deer are harvested each year from each area. While most hunters who frequent these areas like to set up on established trails at field edges and in stands of trees, other hunters move deeper into the marshes. I have hunted both areas (usually with a bow). What many people fail to realize is that deer make trails through the marsh grass and phragmites, as well. A superb marsh hunting technique is to locate an established trail with fresh tracks that lead to an island (really, a raised patched of marshland) and set up just off the trail. Many times, large bucks bed on the dry islands and follow the trails to food sources. While some hunters stay on the ground and use the phragmites as camouflage, other hunters may set up ladders, tri-pod stands, or scaffolding that place them above the phragmites. The same techniques work for salt marshes along the Delaware Bay and the inland bays (like Assawoman) and their tributaries.

As a word of caution, be aware of the tide schedule when hunting a tidal marsh. An easy, though muddy, walk in to a hunting location at low tide may lead to a trudge through knee-high water (or worse) on your walk out. However, remember that deer may follow the pattern of the tides. The dry islands where deer are bedding may only be dry at low tide. Therefore, use the tides to your advantage. High water tends to push deer out of the marsh and into more 'huntable' locations.

As an example of marsh hunting and using the tide to my advantage, I hunted a public deer stand on the edge of the Delaware River during a November 2009 nor-easter. My assumption about deer habits and reaction to incoming tide was correct, although I missed the mark regarding the water levels. I figured the on-shore winds would blow more water into the marsh, thereby forcing deer to leave the islands and move closer to the shore (and toward my stand). This scenario played itself out. Several deer sloshed out of the marsh and made their way to higher ground, though none passed close enough to shoot. Really, I don't think I would have shot anyway because I totally underestimated the power of the storm surge. I walked into my stand (at low tide) before dawn. I stepped through some mud and over a few puddles, but it was no big deal. By 9:00 AM, however, I literally had fish swimming under my stand! No joke! The tide was so high that I was stuck in the stand until the tide receded

Within hours of arriving at the public stand during a 2009 nor-easter, 4 feet of water kept me boxed in.

around 1:00 PM. While this story is somewhat humorous now, the potential dangers are obvious.

Rows of Standing Corn

For Delaware hunters who have permission to hunt farmland, standing cornfields offer an optimal, though much overlooked, location for harvesting quality deer. Cornfields have everything a deer needs – food (corn), cover (the cornstalks), and in some cases water (water can collect in the bottoms of cornstalks or can pool in low spots of the field). It is plain to see why standing cornfields can harbor high numbers of deer.

Just as the cornstalks offer superb cover for deer, they also provide great cover for hunters. With no camouflage, a hunter can walk undetected through rows of corn in order to get close to deer. With good camouflage, a hunter can not only walk through rows of corn without being seen, but he can be standing within mere feet of deer and remain seemingly invisible. On multiple occasions during early season archery hunts I have encountered deer within 10 feet of me when I set up in green, standing corn. Wearing excellent early season camouflage, like Spring Green from Predator, Inc., I once had two does standing within arm's reach of me. They seemingly saw right through me. On another hunt where I was set up on a trail 5 rows deep in a cornfield that bordered a grassy meadow, I witnessed a buck cross the meadow and walk straight to the trail like I wasn't even there. (I still see that buck every day. He's on my office wall.)

Unlike walking through open woods, hunters do not have to worry about stepping on twigs, rustling leaves, or making any other unnatural noises while walking through cornfields. If you have ever heard big deer, especially wide-antlered bucks, walking through corn, you know that they make more racket than an elephant jumping into a leaf pile. With this in mind, remember that cornfields also make good travel routes to other hunting areas. Rather than traveling to your deer stand by walking around field and wood edges where you could potentially be seen by deer, walk through the cornfield so that you remain undetected.

As always, be sure you have proper permission to hunt any agricultural field, public or private, and be aware of any laws or regulations that may prohibit hunting in standing crops. Along the same lines, be familiar with your hunting location. Have a map, a compass, and maybe even a GPS device. Trust me: it is easy to lose your way in a vast maze of 7-foot tall standing corn.

Backyard Hedgerows

One of my favorite places to hunt deer is the vast expanse of Suburbia. While hard to accept by some landowners, others welcome the idea of someone hunting deer in their backyards. After all, Mr. Smith doesn't appreciate that 85% of his landscaping costs are being eaten by deer, and Mrs. Jones can't believe how a collision with one little deer can ruin her SUV. If you can find the Mr. Smiths and Mrs. Joneses who have the land that can safely, legally, and ethically support deer hunting, you can open up a whole new world of hunting opportunities.

I have been hunting suburban backyard deer for years with great success. With my suburban hunting locations close to my home in northern Delaware, they provide quick, alternate hunts when I do not have the time to travel more than 15 minutes to a hunting location. A prime suburban

Tom Bonanno uses backyard hunting techniques to consistently harvest pressured deer.

location on which a friend grants me permission to hunt is everything a deer hunter could ask for. The property consists of several acres of land that slope down to the base of a natural spring. The spring, in turn, flows through a narrow thicket of pine, maple, oak, chestnut, and a few giant sycamore trees, ultimately connecting with a large reservoir. The valley created by the sloping hills and spring offers a phenomenal funnel that deer use daily. Green grass, fallen acorns and chestnuts, and a small spring-fed pool are all natural features that attract deer.

When looking for a hunting location that is off the beaten path, remember to include suburban properties in your search. Ask friends, relatives, and acquaintances, but have a well-thought-out plan first. Be prepared to educate the property owner about applicable hunting laws, provide him with a proposed hunting schedule, and offer to assist her with yard work, especially tasks that will make the property more attractive to deer. Also, be cognizant and respectful of the property's neighbors. They may be against hunting, they may have pets that roam the woods, or they may even be frightened if they see you pull up in your pick-up truck, dressed in camo, and toting a firearm or bow. In instances where neighbors are most likely going to see you, it may be best to ask the property owner to inform them of your intentions. Good relationships with the neighbors can come in handy for several reasons. One, you never know when you may need to track a wounded deer into an adjoining property; and two, it is quite possible that the neighbors are experiencing their own deer problems and may be in need of a skilled hunter to assist them in preserving their shrubbery and vegetable gardens!

Through my experiences, I have learned that many property owners are more inclined to allow you to hunt their land if you use a bow rather than a gun, for obvious reasons. An arrow shot cannot be heard by sleeping residents or neighbors. There is less risk of an arrow traveling into any safety zones or other areas far away from your hunting area. And any anti-gun sentiment is immediately erased. However, still be extremely cautious, since any errors or uses of bad judgment can ruin your hunting privileges (or worse). If hunting with a bow or gun, be sure your aim is true, and avoid any questionable shots. Even deer hit with superb shots (especially with arrows) tend to run before they drop. So be sure to aim for the vitals in an attempt to minimize the distance the wounded deer will travel. You don't want your 10-point buck dying on someone else's property. Likewise, try to minimize the shock value created by dragging your harvest from someone's backyard. Many people are offended, and even more are grossed out by the sight of a deer killed by a hunter. To avoid any possible confrontations, use discretion when gutting deer and loading them into your vehicle.

Techniques

This book is not intended to be a "How to Hunt Deer" guide, and, as such, I will not provide great detail on basic white-tailed deer hunting techniques that apply to deer hunting in most parts of the United States. However, there are certain tried and true techniques that are frequently used with success by Delaware deer hunters. While these techniques may or may not be native to Delaware hunters, they are tactics and methods that best suit the unique challenges associated with deer hunting Delaware's diverse habitats.

Pre-Rut

Hunt Early and Often

With Delaware's deer season opening September 1 for bowhunters, there is no better time to harvest the ultimate white-tailed deer trophy — a buck in velvet. Although some bucks have already lost their velvety antler coverings by September 1, there are many that have not. To increase your chances of harvesting these unique wall-hangers, you must hunt the pre-rut early and often.

Hunting the opening weeks of the Delaware archery deer season is not for everyone. Take it from me: I am all too familiar with 90-plus-degree temperatures, mosquitoes that

Delaware hunter Paul Quigley poses with the ultimate trophy, a pre-rut buck in velvet.

will cause every exposed area of your skin to lump up, and hunting hours that begin before 6:00 AM and end after 7:00 PM. But, it is all worth it when you are the only one amongst your hunting buddies who has the bragging rights associated with harvesting a buck in velvet.

There are relatively few hunters in the woods during the Delaware pre-rut because the first firearms deer season doesn't traditionally begin until early October. The low numbers of hunters coupled with extremely light hunting pressure provide early season hunters with the element of surprise. Since many of the deer haven't seen humans in the woods since January of the previous year, they will be more likely to stick to their normal daily patterns. If you have done some off-season scouting and if you are willing to put in some time in the September heat, you should have success hunting early-season Delaware deer.

Green Camouflage Patterns (Layers)

Much research, hype, and fanfare surround the production and marketing of camouflage patterns. With so many patterns to choose from each season, how can a hunter be sure he is getting the right one? To answer this question, just match your camouflage to the surroundings of your hunting spot and modify it according to the changing seasons.

During the pre-rut period, a good, bright, predominantly green camouflage pattern works best, whether you hunt from a tree stand or on the ground. My personal recommendation is Predator Spring Green camouflage, which works equally well when hunting in green leaves, tall grasses, ragweed, cornstalks, or any other late-summer vegetation. Regardless of which camouflage pattern you choose, remember to play it cool. Wear layers so that you can add or remove clothing as temperatures change, and consider wearing fabrics with moisture-wicking and/or insect repellent properties.

Set Up Near Fresh Water Sources

During early-season, pre-rut hunts, a proven tactic for hunting deer is to set up near freshwater sources that are frequented by deer. I have harvested several pre-rut Delaware bucks and does when hunting near flowing streams, natural springs, and small ponds. During your off-season scouting, consult maps and aerial photos to find fresh water sources near your hunting location. Physically scout the locations and find any well-used trails that lead to the water.

Set-up a stand or build a ground blind in a strategic location where you can intercept deer coming to or from the water source.

This technique works especially well during times of drought. Small water sources may dry up during droughts forcing more deer to move to larger water sources. Therefore, when choosing your hunting location near a water source, be aware that it could disappear in mid-season.

Hunt from the Ground

With so much foliage in the woods and fields during the early, pre-rut period, it makes sense to hunt from the ground. Hunting from the ground gives you the ability to adapt, since you can move closer to deer, move to get a better shot angle, or move to better match your surroundings.

As mentioned above, be sure to have a camouflage pattern that adequately matches your surroundings before hunting from the ground. When hunting from a tree stand, you can get away with more motion, noise, and scent when deer are close. However, when you are on the ground, you are closer to a deer's eyes, ears, and nose, so good camouflage is crucial.

Perhaps the most important thing to remember when hunting from the ground is to use the wind to your advantage. When you have a general idea of where you want to hunt and you think you know where the deer are, be sure to approach the location from an angle where the wind will not blow your scent toward the deer. It cannot be stressed enough that you should *never compromise your wind*. Above all else, most big bucks do not come within shooting range

Hunting from the ground gives you the ability to adapt, since you can move closer to deer, move to get a better shot angle, or move to better match your surroundings.

because they are spooked by strange scents. This is an important rule to follow even if you use 'scent-free' clothing.

Bug-Proof Your Clothing

If I had a nickel for every tick I pulled off my body and a penny for every mosquito that bit me during my pre-rut hunts I would be a billionaire. Well, maybe not, but you get the point.

With documented cases of Lyme disease, Rocky Mountain spotted fever, eastern equine encephalitis, and West Nile virus occurring in Delaware and the surrounding areas, it is imperative to make your clothes (and body) as bug-proof as possible during early season hunts. (Actually, this principal holds true for all times of the hunting season, but ticks and mosquitoes are especially bad before the first frost of the hunting season.) Wear specially treated clothing, spray your clothes with insect repellent, tuck your pants into your boots, and wear hats, masks, and gloves to combat the numerous critters that see your blood as a tasty meal. If you are worried about the scent created by insect repellents that are applied to your clothes and skin, spray your clothes several days in advance and let them air-out before wearing them. There are several heavy-duty insect repellents on the market that are made specifically for application to clothing.

Rut

Stay All Day

When hunting Delaware deer during the rut, be prepared to stay at your hunting spot all day. Whether you are hunting public or private land with a gun or with a bow, your chances of harvesting a buck during the rut are greater if you hunt the mid-day hours in addition to morning and afternoon hours.

Many hunters traditionally hunt the morning from sunrise to about 10:00 AM, then they head back to the truck for a sandwich and nap. After their nap and a lukewarm cup of coffee from their thermoses, they head back to their deer stands around 2:00 PM.

The crafty Delaware hunter, on the other hand, packs his sandwich and coffee with him to the stand and stays in his stand all day. He is waiting for the morning and afternoon hunters to walk out of and in to the woods with hopes that they spook deer right to him. Likewise, he knows that there are no predictable deer during the rut. Deer will break free from their normal patterns, and their hormones will drive them toward hot does at any time of day, be it morning, noon, or night.

Realizing that boredom sets in and nature inevitably calls for you to leave your stand, use these opportunities to continue to hunt. Assuming you are legally allowed to hunt from the ground (some Delaware hunting rules mandate that you hunt from a stand during certain seasons at certain locations), bring your bow or loaded gun with you when you take a short walk. Always be aware of your surroundings and remain stealthy because you could very easily encounter deer.

Change Your Location (Find the Does)

If you are targeting bucks during the rut, do not assume that they will follow their same pre-rut patterns. As just about every human male can attest to, hormones make us do crazy things. Deer are no different. They will let their hormones dictate their behavior.

With this being said, it is a good idea to abandon your pre-rut hunting location during the rut. Instead, set up where you know does and family groups of deer frequent. During the rut, if you find the does, you will inevitably find some bucks. Just keep in mind that in addition to a wary buck keeping an eye out for you, you may have to contend with the numerous eyes of does, yearlings, and fawns.

Hunt Scrapes

I had my doubts about hunting near buck scrapes until I witnessed firsthand a buck go berserk when I made a mock scrape next to his. I erroneously thought that bucks would make scrapes every so often, then possibly come back to refresh them once or twice. I had no idea that some bucks actually guard their scrapes!

On the second day of the 2006 Delaware shotgun season, in the heart of the rut, I decided to bowhunt one of my locations in Suburbia. Thinking that public land pressure from shotgun hunters would push deer onto this private paradise paid off. Walking to my stand, I noticed a buck scrape on the ground, about 10 yards from my tree stand. Using my boot heel, I made a mock scrape next to the real buck scrape. I dripped a drop or two of interdigital scent into my mock scrape and sprayed buck urine into it. I also sprayed some buck urine on the surrounding branches and got up in my stand about 3:00 PM.

By 3:10 PM, a buck walked right up behind my stand and bedded down 15 yards away! After straining my neck to peek around my tree, I saw the buck lying there. Its rack was three points on one side and a broken antler on the other. It bedded there for about 45 minutes then walked farther back into the

The author Steven Kendus with an 8-point backyard buck harvested over a mock scrape during the heart of the rut.

woods. At about 4:15, I figured I would test my grunting ability in an attempt to get the buck to come back. Within 30 seconds of my grunting, an 8-point buck came out of nowhere! He ran down a hill in front of my stand, and came straight to my mock scrape! Man, did he look upset. He was stomping and snorting, and then he went about refreshing his initial scrape right next to the one I made. He pawed and scratched, and then he stood over the scrape and emptied his bladder into it. After all that showmanship, he walked right to where I sprayed the scent on a branch, which was right in my shooting lane. As he walked behind a tree, I came to full draw. He stepped out, sniffed the air, and grunted as I let the arrow fly. The arrow hit true, right in the heart. He ran 15 yards and dropped.

Smell Like a Deer

As you can see from my buck scrape story above, I am a believer and avid user of cover scents and deer attractant scents. While I have used 'scent-free' suits with activated charcoal, I cannot say that I am convinced that they lead to more successful hunts. I have harvested just as many deer with the 'scent-free' suit as without it. Rather than attempting to totally eliminate my natural human scent, I think it is more important to make myself smell like a deer or something else in a deer's world that is pleasing (or at least not alarming) to his nose.

I take precautions in that I wash my clothes in scent-free detergent, I bathe with scent-free soaps, and I try not to enter the woods smelling like I just came off a shift as head fry cook at a local diner. I also make sure that I spray my hunting boots with a cover scent prior to walking into my hunting location. Depending on time of year, hunting location, and weather conditions, I will spray my boots with raccoon or fox urine, earth scent, or doe urine. Additionally, I may drip a drop or two of deer interdigital scent directly on the soles of my boots. I may also spray my clothes with a charcoal-containing scent eliminator and/or various cover scents that smell like deer, vanilla, leaves, berries, or corn. To top things off, I will spray some deer attractant scent near my deer stand or ground location in strategic spots. I apply them sparingly to objects (leaves, stumps, branches, etc.) in shooting lanes where I want deer to stop.

Chris Antonio with an 11-point monster harvested in Sussex County, Delaware during the rut.

Post-Rut

Move to a Tree

While there still may be some foliage left on trees during the early post-rut period, most of the trees' leaves have browned and/or dropped. When hunting the post-rut woods in Delaware (especially during December and January), a good practice is to hunt from a tree stand. Even most hunters who traditionally hunt from the ground during the pre-rut and rut periods will agree that the wide open winter woods makes it more difficult to hunt from the ground.

Still hunting, where a hunter stealthily stalks and frequently pauses, is a viable option, but fewer leaves for camouflage and tons of dried leaves that crackle with every step create additional challenges. As always, put some research into optimal stand placement so that you can maximize your chances for harvesting a Delaware deer. Deer will begin to herd together during the post-rut period, so finding the bedding, feeding, or traveling area of one deer usually means finding multiple deer. Strategically place your stand on established trails or field edges where deer tracks are prevalent, but be sure to keep shooting distances in mind. If hunting with a bow, you need to set up relatively close to the terrain feature you are hunting (i.e. trails, bedding areas, feeding areas), whereas if you are hunting with a gun, you can setup in a location where you may be able to cover multiple terrain features from one position.

Also, if possible, have multiple stands set up. Again, since deer tend to herd together during the post-rut period, oftentimes hunting tends to be "all or nothing." You may have an entire herd of twenty-plus deer walk past your stand, or you may have a whopping zero deer walk past your stand. However, if luck is on your side and you happen to see a herd of deer in another location, it may make sense for you to sneak to another stand location that is closer to the herd.

Hunt Feeding Areas (or Create Your Own)

During the cold post-rut months of December and January, Delaware deer herds will be on seemingly constant searches for food. Knowing this, a successful post-rut hunter will — like a deer — conduct his own searches for deer food sources. After locating the food sources, such as fallen nuts, unharvested crops, and any leftover green foliage, he will strategically set up deer stands or ground blinds on well-used deer trails that lead to the food sources. Using this post-rut strategy, it is only a matter of time before a shot presents itself.

In addition to hunting wild food sources, hunters who hunt on private land in Delaware can create their own food sources for deer. As of the writing of this book, Delaware hunting regulations allow hunters to hunt deer over bait on private land.[21] While some may view hunting deer over bait as unethical, it is just one more tool used by the State of Delaware to control the growing deer population. Typically, feed corn is used for deer bait, but I have also seen apples, birdseed, farm animal feed mixes, sorghum, and other natural baits used. Some private land deer hunters in Delaware use elaborate, solar-powered feeders that throw out feed at set intervals, while others just dump bags, wheelbarrows, or truckloads full of feed into piles.

Hunt the Weather

Through research and experience, I have concluded that deer have an uncanny way of sensing when the weather is about to take a turn for the worse. If deer can sense that rain, snow, or severe cold is on the horizon, they may feed more heavily than normal. Although few of us have that same uncanny weather sense of a deer, we have the benefits of the local news, The Weather Channel, and the Internet. Therefore, pay attention to the weather forecast during deer hunting season.

---

[21] *2010-2011 Delaware Hunting & Trapping Guide*, 7.

Paul Quigley knows that post-rut hunts, while potentially cold, can be productive.

Hunt the leading edges of weather fronts and systems that will provide any disruption to a deer's normal patterns. For example, if the forecast is calling for a snowstorm to begin on Wednesday, hunt Tuesday and Wednesday, right up until the storm hits. Sensing that food supplies and movement may be limited by snow and cold, deer will tend to feed heavily before the storm hits. Before forecasted foul weather, situate yourself near feeding areas or on trails that directly lead to feeding areas for increased chances of harvesting a Delaware post-rut deer.

Along the same lines, be sure to hunt immediately after storms. Just as deer may feed heavily in anticipation of a storm, they may also be more inclined to search for food after a storm passes. During wind, rain, sleet, and snow storms, deer tend to move less and may even bed down. If a storm lasts for a day or more, they will be on the move in search of food after it ends.

Bring Enough Ammo

Since the post-rut period provides hunters with their last opportunities for filling their seasonal tags, it is important to bring enough ammunition to the field! I know this sounds like basic common sense, but it is conceivable that a herd of deer could walk by your stand and present you with multiple shots. Considering the fact that you could have all of your deer tags left and that your uncle, neighbor, and friend at work all want venison, you may need more than a few shells or arrows.

Delaware hunting licenses typically include two doe-only tags and two antlerless tags. Additionally, Hunter's Choice tags are usually available for $10, which allows hunters to use the tags on an antlerless or antlered deer. The Hunter's Choice tag includes a Quality Buck Tag that allows the owner to tag a buck with a minimum outside spread of 15 inches.

Curt Barkus, dressed in appropriate snow camouflage, hunts the day after a winter snowstorm.

With the possibility for six tags (plus as many additional doe tags as needed, since they are also available for $10 each), it is conceivable that a hunter could fill a bunch of tags in a single day. With a standard box of shotgun slugs holding five slugs, it is important that the number of boxes carried into the woods match your deer hunting goals. Likewise, for bowhunters, make sure that you carry enough arrows in your quiver to cover your harvest goals, as well as any missed and unrecovered shots.

This section probably strikes many as strange. However, in my youth and inexperience, I thought I was infallible as a bowhunter and only carried a quiver of three arrows. During an after-work Pennsylvania bowhunt near a friend's house, yes, I ran out of arrows. I was in a climbing stand, set up near a flowing stream. Two does walked by early, so I decided I would take one because I was more than an hour from home and didn't want to get stuck tracking a deer after dark. I drew on the doe, who was standing still, and let the arrow fly. The arrow hit a branch 2 feet in front of me, and kicked downward, missing the deer by 10 feet. The two does ran away. Realizing that I was in prime deer hunting time, I didn't risk making noise climbing down to retrieve the arrow.

About 15 minutes later, I saw a buck walking toward the stream. He drank for a while, and then began walking straight up the trail in front of my stand. I drew and waited for him to come in my shooting lane. When he did, I whistled and he stopped. I let the arrow fly, but as I squeezed the trigger on my release, the buck hunched down, and (unknowingly to me) the arrow hit him high. The deer immediately fell. Thinking he was mortally wounded, I lowered my bow to my side. As I moved, the deer looked directly up at me, got up, and took off running. I used my last arrow to attempt a second shot him, but the arrow sailed wide into a thicket of honeysuckle. I waited about fifteen minutes and climbed down to track the buck. I saw where he ran, I heard him crash through branches, and I had a good blood trail to follow. I followed the trail for about 10 minutes and found the buck backed into a thicket and small ravine — still alive.

Because of his precarious position, he could see me. Any move I made toward him, he tried to lunge at me with his antlers. He didn't have the strength to pull himself out of the ravine, and I didn't have any arrows to quickly end his suffering. Using my mobile phone, I called my friend whose house backed up to the woods where I was. He ran out with his bow and put a final shot on the buck. Because of my inexperience, cockiness, and poor judgment, I learned valuable lessons. I never think I am infallible, and I now take a bigger quiver and more arrows to the field with me.

3

Wild Turkey Hunting

Relatively few hunters pursue wild turkeys in Delaware, but those hunters who do are passionate about turkey hunting. With recent increases in wild turkey numbers in Delaware, turkey hunting is gaining popularity. Subsequently, more first-time turkey hunters are taking to the Delaware woods each spring in pursuit of wild gobblers.

About Delaware Turkeys

Although the Delaware wild turkey population was considered to be wiped out by over-hunting from the mid-1800s until 1984 (when they were reintroduced to the wild by the Delaware Division of Fish & Wildlife), they are now thriving in many parts of the state and, subsequently, are considered prized game by many Delaware hunters. Recent estimates put the size of the Delaware turkey flock near 4,000 birds, thanks to efforts by the National Wild Turkey Federation, neighboring states, and the Delaware Division of Fish & Wildlife.[22] Wild turkeys were initially re-introduced to Delaware in Sussex County at Milford Neck Wildlife Area

---

[22] Delaware Division of Fish and Wildlife. *Peek-A-Boo I See Turkeys; 4,000 Wild Turkeys since 1986, A Restoration Success Story.*

Author Steven Kendus carries a 17.5-pound jake with a nine-inch beard through an early spring field.

and at Cypress Swamp near Dagsboro, but now wild turkeys can be found in New Castle, Kent, and Sussex Counties.

Habitat and Food

The eastern wild turkey, the turkey species native to Delaware, thrives in Delaware's diverse landscape. Turkey flocks, which can consist of just a few birds to fifty or more birds, prefer forested habitats with nearby access to food and water sources. Turkey flocks may establish home ranges of several thousand acres, so Delaware's forested areas, agricultural fields, stream and river banks, and pond edges offer turkeys prime locations for continuing their strong comeback.

Turkeys are omnivorous, in that they eat both plant and animal foods. Depending on seasonal availability, wild turkeys eat nuts, acorns, tender leaves, fruits, seeds, berries, and flowers, as well as insects, worms, grubs, and other invertebrates. Like the familiar images of feeding barnyard chickens, turkeys frequently scratch up the ground and "hunt and peck" in search of food.

Physical Characteristics

To new turkey hunters, seeing wild turkeys up close for the first time is astounding. Many hunters cannot believe how big the birds actually are, and they are quite intrigued by the iridescent, seemingly plastic-like look of their feathers. Mature male turkeys, called "toms" or "gobblers" stand close to three-feet tall and can weigh more than 25 pounds, although the average weight is closer to 17 pounds. (In fact, a Delaware state record turkey was harvested during the 2007 spring turkey season that weighed more than 27 pounds.) Immature (less than two years old) males, called "jakes", are usually smaller, although I have personally harvested a 17.5-pound jake.

A rare trophy, this New Jersey jake has five beards.

Typically, both gobblers and jakes have beards, hair-like bunches of bristles that protrude from their upper breasts. Male turkeys usually have one beard, although it is not uncommon to encounter turkeys with two, three, or more beards. (As a testament to multi-bearded turkeys, I harvested a jake with five beards during New Jersey's 2007 spring turkey season.) Beards vary in length and thickness, ranging from a few inches to more than 12 inches in length. Although not a true way to gauge the age of a male turkey, jakes usually have shorter, thinner beards than gobblers. Another characteristic that distinguishes jakes from gobblers is the set of tail feathers, also known as the fan. The central tail feathers of jake fans are longer than the rest of the tail feathers, creating an uneven semi-circle when displayed. By contrast, gobbler tail feathers are uniform in length and create an even semi-circle when displayed.

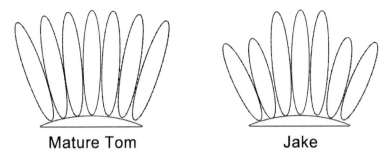

Mature Tom   Jake

Mature tom tail feathers are uniform in length and create an even semi-circle. Jake central tail feathers are longer than the rest of the tail feathers, creating an uneven semi-circle.

The body feathers of male turkeys are dark brown and black, but give off iridescent hues of blue, green, orange, and tan. Their tail feathers are predominantly chestnut brown, with black striations, and tan and black tips. Gobblers and jakes typically have bald, light blue and red heads and thorn-like spurs on the backs of their legs.

Female turkeys, called "hens", are about half the size of mature gobblers. As with most female birds, turkey hens' feathers are duller than those of males. Their feathers are a lighter brown, and their heads are not bald, like males. Instead, the heads of female turkeys are covered in tiny, hair-like feathers. In most cases, turkey hens do not have beards or spurs.

Turkey Sounds

Just as hunters are amazed at the size of wild turkeys, they are equally impressed by the thunderous volume of the male turkey's gobble. Turkeys make an interesting array of sounds, but the gobble, by far, is the sound that most appeals to a turkey hunter. When a gobbler or jake is close, the "gobble-gobble-gobble-gobble-gobble-gobble" in response to a hen yelp is unmistakable.

I remember my first turkey hunt when I first heard the gobbles of two nearby turkeys. At first I thought the gobbles were being made by another hunter. They sounded too much like what I heard on TV newscasts around Thanksgiving time. However, after realizing that the gobbles were getting closer and louder with each hen yelp I made, I realized they were the real thing. It took everything I had to calm down, stop shaking, and actually squeeze the trigger when the first bird stepped into range!

Imitating a male turkey's gobble while hunting is not advisable, since other hunters tend to key in on gobbles. However, imitating turkey hens in search of a mate is the most effective way of calling in male turkeys. Turkey hens yelp, cluck, purr, cut, cackle, and putt depending on their communication needs and locations. They may yelp loudly to attract attention, cluck to attract other birds, purr softly just before flying down from a tree in the morning, cackle while flying, or putt to issue warnings. A well-prepared turkey hunter will know how to imitate these calls and will know in which situations to use them.

Do Turkeys Really Fly?

You bet they do—and pretty darn fast, too! Turkeys can fly at speeds in excess of 45 miles per hour for distances up to a mile. Not bad for a twenty-plus-pound bird. Although turkeys can fly quite well, they usually run from danger.

Turkeys can run at speeds in excess of 15 miles per hour, with strides over three feet! Suffice it to say, if you happen to scare that nice gobbler you were hunting and cause him to take off running, chances are you will not catch him (especially when he can still fly if he feels really threatened).

Turkey Roosts

While flocks of wild turkeys spend most of their days walking the forest floor and surrounding clearings in search of food and water, they roost in trees at night. Typically, individual turkeys of a flock will fly up to tree branches in close proximity to other members of the flock at dusk, and will fly down around dawn.

If a turkey hunter can accurately determine the location of a turkey roost, he can greatly increase his chances of success. Setting up near the roost area before dawn enables the hunter to possibly encounter the turkeys as they fly down and reassemble for the day. In some cases though, this method of hunting may prove too close for comfort. In the spring of 2007, I hunted a turkey roost. I saw the flock walk into a patch of woods just before dusk, so I figured they would roost in a nearby stand of tall trees. So the next morning I set up in the woods 90 minutes before dawn, trying to guess the precise location of the roost. At dawn, I began calling. To my surprise, I heard no return calls. Finding this puzzling, I assessed the situation. I looked up, and I realized I was surrounded by the entire flock of turkeys! They were roosted in about five trees all around me. They saw me walk in, saw me set up, and saw me call. There was no way they were going to fly down anywhere near me. After two hours, the birds flew down, but they landed and assembled about 200 yards from me.

Delaware Turkey Hunting Season

After the successful reintroduction of wild turkeys to Delaware, the State offered its first wild turkey hunting season in 1991. Although wild turkey hunting is relatively new to Delaware, it is slowly beginning to catch on with hunters who have traditionally only hunted deer and waterfowl in Delaware. Although some neighboring states offer separate spring and fall turkey hunting seasons, Delaware currently only offers a spring season. Usually running for about 3 weeks from mid-April to early May, hunters are provided with adequate time to bag a gobbler. The eastern wild turkey typically begins breeding in early spring, so by the time the Delaware turkey season arrives, mature male turkeys are actively competing for mates and are more apt to respond to the hen decoys and calls of turkey hunters.

With strict harvest limits in place, Delaware ensures the continued success of their overall turkey flock. Currently, only bearded birds may be harvested, and most importantly, only one turkey per year may be harvested per hunter. Typically, bearded birds are thought to be only gobblers or jakes, but be aware that some turkey hens may rarely sport beards.

Turkey Hunting Safety Class

As of the printing of this book, all first-time Delaware turkey hunters must take a Turkey Hunting Safety class before actually hunting turkeys. The Delaware Division of Fish and Wildlife's Hunter Education Program provides the course so that all Delaware turkey hunters are aware of the specific dangers inherent with turkey hunting, as well as the methods and techniques that increase the hunters' chances of success.

Because a turkey's eyes are extremely sharp, hunters must use exceptional camouflage and concealment to increase their chances of harvesting a turkey. When you combine this camouflage and concealment with decoys, calling, and other hunters, there is potential for ruined hunts, in-the-field arguments, and ultimately, misdirected shots. As with all hunting, safety should be a turkey hunter's first priority, and the Delaware Division of Fish & Wildlife is taking the necessary steps to promote safe turkey hunting.

Public Land Hunting Permits

If you have the luxury of hunting wild turkeys on private land, you can hunt for the entire spring season (or until you bag your bird). However, if you intend to hunt wild turkeys on Delaware public land, you must apply for a turkey hunting permit, for which the application is available from the annual *Delaware Hunting & Trapping Guide*. When submitting the application for a public land turkey hunting permit, you must choose preferred locations and preferred hunting dates. For public land turkey hunting, the spring turkey season is typically broken into three or four segments.

Delaware public lands traditionally open to wild turkey hunting include:

- Assawoman Wildlife Area - Sussex County
- Blackbird State Forest - New Castle and Kent Counties
- Blackiston Wildlife Area – New Castle and Kent Counties
- Cedar Swamp Wildlife Area – New Castle County
- C&D Canal Wildlife Area – New Castle County
- Industrial Forest Wildlife Area – Sussex County
- Little Creek Wildlife Area – Kent County
- Marshy Hope Wildlife Area – Sussex County
- Midlands Wildlife Area – Sussex County
- Milford Neck Wildlife Area - Kent and Sussex Counties
- Nanticoke Wildlife Area – Sussex County
- Norman G. Wilder Wildlife Area – Kent County
- Old Furnace Wildlife Area – Sussex County
- Prime Hook National Wildlife Refuge – Sussex County
- Redden State Forest/Taber forest including Barr Tract – Sussex County
- Ted Harvey Wildlife Area /Buckaloo – Kent County
- Ted Harvey Wildlife Area/Logan Lane - Kent County
- Urban/Forney Wildlife Area – Kent County
- Woodland Beach Wildlife Area – Kent County

Turkey Hunting Methods

Although, like deer hunting, the vast majority of Delaware turkey hunting is done with a shotgun, hunters who seek additional challenges may also hunt turkeys with a muzzleloader or bow.

Shotgun

When most hunters think of wild turkey hunting, they easily recall images from Saturday morning television shows where hunters are using the latest in camouflage-coated shotguns to stealthily bag their birds. The latest in shotgun

Delaware hunter Evan Grabowski harvested this 21-pound Delaware gobbler on public land in Kent County, Delaware. The tom had a 10 3/4-inch beard and 3/4-inch spurs.

design is good, but in reality, any functional shotgun of sufficient gauge, with the appropriate choke tube, and the appropriate ammunition is capable of taking down a big gobbler.

As established in the 2010-2011 *Delaware Hunting & Trapping Guide*, Delaware hunting regulations dictate that 20-, 16-, 12-, and 10-gauge shotguns may be used for hunting wild turkeys, and legal shot can be lead or steel in sizes 4, 5, or 6.[23] The gauge of the shotgun used is personal preference, but 12- and 10-gauge guns are most commonly used because of their increased knockdown power and range. Since a properly placed shotgun shot at a turkey is on the head and neck area, it important to use a choke tube that holds the shot pattern close together at the ranges where you will be shooting the large birds. Specially designed, screw-in choke tubes are manufactured and marketed specifically for turkey hunting, but as with all guns, proper sighting-in and practice are crucial. Practice shooting your shotgun at turkey head/neck targets (available for purchase from gun and sporting goods shops and available for free on the Internet) at different distances. Try to make your practice shooting situations mimic as closely as possible actual hunting conditions. Since most turkey shooting is done from a seated position, practice shooting while sitting on your rear-end and while kneeling.

When choosing a shotgun for turkey hunting, there are several factors to consider in addition to gauge and choke. A plain-Jane, blued, pump-action shotgun with wood forearm and stock and standard iron sights is a sufficient gun for harvesting a turkey. But, as with all hunting, there are ways to increase your chances of success. Rather than blued metal, consider purchasing a shotgun that covers all exposed metal, wood, and composite material in camouflage so that light reflections are minimized. Consider purchasing a semi-automatic shotgun, so that you can quickly fire a second or

---

[23] *Delaware Hunting & Trapping Guide*, 27.

third shot if needed. Likewise, consider enhancing the standard sights by adding fiber-optic or holographic sights that enable you to draw a bead on a turkey more quickly and accurately. Other options to consider include lighter weight for enhanced maneuverability, comfortable sling for easy carrying, and adjustable shooting sticks or bipods that can provide additional support and shot accuracy.

Archery

Hunting turkeys with a bow may be one of the most challenging hunts an archer will encounter. Turkeys present much smaller areas for successful shot placement when compared with the vital organ areas of large mammals like deer, and their keen vision makes it extremely difficult to draw a bowstring when turkeys are in range. However, with enough practice, patience, and luck, harvesting a Delaware gobbler with a bow is not impossible.

The 2010-2011 *Delaware Hunting & Trapping Guide* establishes that turkeys may be hunted with longbows or compound bows with arrows that have a broadhead of at least 7/8 of an inch.[24] Many successful bow hunters use mechanical broadheads for hunting turkeys because of their accuracy and wide cutting diameters. Since pinpoint accuracy is needed when targeting a turkey's wing butt, hip joint, heart, neck, or head with an arrow, the extra cutting diameter of a mechanical broadhead allows a little forgiveness for a shot that is a bit off the mark. Some broadheads on the market are tipped with long, fixed blades that extend perpendicular from the arrow shaft. The blades, which provide cutting diameters up to four inches, are meant to be shot at a turkey's

---

[24] *Delaware Hunting & Trapping Guide*, 27.

Delawarean Tom Morganstern enjoys the added challenge of hunting gobblers with a bow.

neck so that the head is completely removed from the body, effectively dropping the bird in its tracks.

To increase your chances of harvesting a Delaware turkey with a bow, you absolutely must practice, practice, and practice some more. Practice shooting baseball-sized targets at distances up to 30 yards, and practice drawing and shooting your bow from your knee(s). If you will be hunting from a blind, practice shooting from the blind, through every window where you could possibly launch an arrow. Try to practice in conditions that most closely resemble your actual hunting environment. As an example, I frequently bowhunt turkeys from a blind in which I sit in a wooden chair. To maximize my odds, I practice drawing and shooting from the chair.

Muzzleloader

Using a muzzleloader for turkey hunting can be just as effective as using a shotgun on Delaware gobblers, though a bit more challenging. Delaware hunting regulations stipulate that smoothbore muzzleloading shotguns (i.e. muzzleloaders with shotgun barrels) with number 4, 5, or 6 shot may be used for hunting turkeys.[25] With a smoothbore muzzleloading shotgun having many of the same shooting characteristics of a regular shotgun, it is easy to see how a muzzleloader can be used effectively on a gobbler. A dense pattern of pellets striking a gobbler's head and neck have the same effect whether they came from a muzzleloading shotgun or a regular shotgun.

Because muzzleloaders can only be fired once (or twice with a double-barrel model) before reloading, there is increased pressure to make sure the first shot counts. Also, as mentioned in the muzzleloader section in the White-tailed

---

[25] *Delaware Hunting & Trapping Guide*, 27.

Deer Hunting chapter of this book, there are increased risks of mechanical failure when hunting with a muzzleloader. It is important to be familiar with all operational aspects of your muzzleloader before heading to the field, and it is imperative that you sight in and pattern your muzzleloader before hunting with it. Be sure to test varying loads, shot sizes, and shot cups (if you use them), since they can all affect the pattern and effective range of your shot. Likewise, as with hunting with a shotgun, practice shooting your muzzleloader at turkey head/neck targets at different distances, and practice shooting from seated and kneeling positions.

When selecting a muzzleloader for turkey hunting, consider options similar to those available for regular shotguns. Consider lightweight, composite materials, camouflage coatings, fiber-optic or holographic sights, a comfortable sling, and adjustable shooting sticks or bipods. For details regarding the differences between inline muzzleloaders and primitive (flintlock and percussion) muzzleloaders, refer to the aforementioned muzzleloader section within this book's White-tailed Deer Hunting chapter.

Turkey Hunting Hotspots

One of the most common questions I hear is "Where can I find turkeys in Delaware?" Seasoned Delaware turkey hunters and bird watchers alike have pretty good ideas of the locations where turkeys frequent, but many novice hunters don't even know where to begin searching. After all, if you are not actively looking for wild turkeys, they can be pretty tough to spot. Although they are big birds, they can be well camouflaged. Tall grasses and thick underbrush easily hide the birds. Additionally, to the unknowing eye, they can be easily mistaken for turkey vultures or black vultures as they walk through roadside fields in search of food. Many people drive past flocks of feeding turkeys every day and don't even realize they are looking at wild turkeys. However, as a hunter in search of traditional Thanksgiving table fare or a full-mounted gobbler in full strut, it is necessary to recognize the prime Delaware turkey hunting locations.

Hot Turkey Management Zones

I have personally witnessed wild turkeys in New Castle, Kent, and Sussex Counties, but the majority of the Delaware flock seems to be located in the lower two-thirds of the state. According to statistics from the Delaware Division of Fish & Wildlife, during the 2009 spring turkey hunting season, 312 turkeys were harvested in Delaware, up 25% from the 2008 harvest of 249 birds and up 75% from the 2007 harvest of 178 birds. Two hundred eighty-one (90%) of the birds were taken on private land, compared to only 31 birds from Delaware public hunting areas. Turkey management zones 6 and 11 produced the most turkeys, and zones 1 and 3 produced the fewest. Turkeys were harvested in all turkey management zones, except zone 1. [26]

When seeking a hot turkey management zone to hunt, refer to the statistics mentioned above. With zones 6, 11, and 12 each producing good harvests (from public and private land), you can conclude that there is a high number of birds in those areas. If you have permission to hunt private land in those zones, begin planning next season's hunt! If not, consult a Delaware map, and take a drive through prime turkey

---

[26] Project Statement, Delaware – Grant W38R-10, Wildlife Investigations – Wild Turkey, 2.

hunting territory. If you find private land that looks appealing, try to locate and contact the land owner to ask permission to hunt. If you cannot gain hunting privileges on private land, request Redden State Forest and/or Norman G. Wilder Wildlife Management Area on your Delaware application for a public land turkey hunting permit.

Turkey Harvested on Delaware Public Lands (2009)[27]

Public Hunting Area	Number of Turkey Harvested	Turkey Management Zone	County
Redden State Forest	9	8,11,12,15	Sussex
Norman G. Wilder WMA	7	6	Kent
Blackbird Reserve, Blackbird Sate Forest	4	2	New Castle, Kent
Little Creek WMA	3	5	Kent
Milford Neck WMA	1	9	Kent, Sussex
Blackiston WMA	1	4	Kent
Midlands WMA	1	14	Sussex
Nanticoke WMA	1	13	Sussex
Old Furnace WMA	1	11	Sussex
Taber State Forest	1	7	Kent
Urban/Fortney Tracts	1	4	Kent
Woodland Beach WMA	1	5	Kent

[27] Project Statement, Delaware – Grant W38R-10, Wildlife Investigations – Wild Turkey, 4.

Techniques

Since Delaware's spring turkey season only lasts for about three or four weeks, a turkey hunter should do as much as possible to maximize his chances of harvesting a gobbler. Presented below are some techniques, tips, and tactics that my hunting buddies and I have used to harvest wild turkeys in Delaware (as well as New Jersey, Maryland, and Pennsylvania).

Scouting is Crucial

Although Delaware's overall turkey numbers are increasing, it still can be difficult to find turkeys during hunting season. To maximize your limited hunting time and to increase your chances of success, it is imperative to scout your available hunting areas prior to pinpointing an exact hunting location. While a bad day of hunting beats a good day at work, none of us wants to get up at 3:30 AM, head out to the woods, and not see or hear a turkey all day.

Several weeks before the opening of the turkey season, take some drives or walks through the areas you are considering hunting. Look for turkeys and turkey signs (like tracks, feathers, and scratch marks) and take mental notes of possible places to hunt in close proximity to the turkeys. Be sure to scout in the morning and evening to get good ideas of feeding and roosting patterns and locations. After several scouting trips, you can determine the best locations for setting up.

I have found that scouting the night before a hunt can be extremely productive. As mentioned earlier, turkeys roost in trees at night. If you can remain undetected while scouting turkeys at dusk, you can determine with a fair amount of

Pre-season scouting for turkey sign, like these turkey tracks, can increase your chances of bagging a big gobbler.

accuracy where they are roosting. If you know where they are roosting for the night, you can set up in close proximity to them and hope to catch them the next morning.

Camo is Key

As with hunting deer, it is imperative that turkey hunters match their camouflage to the surroundings of their hunting spots and modify it according to the changing seasons. In fact, with turkeys having eyesight that may be better than a deer's and with hunters usually sitting on the ground at the turkey's eye level, it is probably *more* important for a turkey hunter to have sufficient camouflage.

Spring camouflage can be tricky because Delaware's flora can change quickly. At the beginning of the hunting season, a predominantly leafy brown camouflage pattern may be good. However, during the last week of the season when new leaves are exploding, a bright, predominantly green camouflage pattern may work best. Whichever camouflage pattern you choose, be sure to cover as much of your body as possible in order to break up your silhouette and eliminate any drastic color differences and glare. Cover your face with a mask or net, and be sure your hands are covered with gloves. Turkeys are easily frightened by movement that they cannot easily identify, so adequate camouflage alone is not enough. It is also important to remain as still as possible when turkeys are present.

While we are discussing clothing, it is important to point out that it is never a good idea to wear any clothing (or to have anything in your possession) while turkey hunting that has the colors red, white or blue. Because turkey heads and feathers include shades of red, white, and blue, it is dangerous to wear such colors. In fact, Delaware hunting guidelines dictate that it is illegal to wear any visible garments that include the colors red, white, or blue while turkey hunting.[28]

Arrive Early

Why is it that we hunters hate the horrible buzz of the alarm clock when it wakes us up on workdays, but we love its sound when it wakes us up to hunt? Whatever the answer, a

---

[28] *Delaware Hunting & Trapping Guide*, 27.

Well camouflaged, Joycee Morganstern proves that turkey hunting is a sport that is also enjoyed by women.

true turkey hunter knows that the alarm clock can be his best friend.

Because wild turkeys tend to leave their roosts just after dawn, it is a good practice to arrive at your hunting spot well before dawn. In my case, I try to arrive one-and-a-half to two hours prior to sunrise, which typically equates to some time around 4:30 AM during mid-spring. If you have done a good job of scouting the night before your hunt, you will have a pretty good idea of where your turkeys will be roosting. Since they will be roosted above you, it is important to walk to your hunting spot under the cover of darkness. Deer, foxes, raccoons, and other animals roam the woods at night, so your walking through the woods will not necessarily scare the turkeys. However, be sure to make as little noise as possible, use as little light as possible, and get to your spot and get set up as quickly as possible.

After getting situated, try to remain still and quiet. Listen intently for turkey calls, since the birds will sometimes call to each other before it gets light. If you hear turkeys and they sound close to you, don't call since they may see you. Instead, wait for daylight to see if you can pinpoint the birds' locations. However, if you hear birds calling and they sound relatively far away, move closer to them as quickly as possible. Use your discretion before moving locations, but do not hesitate to reposition yourself if you have adequate time.

Along the same lines, always remember to face the gobbles. Regardless of where your decoys are set up or where you think the turkeys will show up, always try to reposition yourself so that you are facing the gobbles. I was turkey hunting one opening morning and heard gobbles almost immediately after legal shooting time. I was set up about 10 yards deep in the woods with my back against a tree and facing the edge of a plowed field. I set up two decoys in the field and assumed the turkeys would walk out into the field where I saw them the day before. My confidence turned to disgust as two big toms walked 10 feet behind my tree but never walked out to the field or anywhere within my shooting lanes. If I would have just repositioned myself by moving to the other side of the tree, I could have caught the turkeys walking toward me. Instead, I left empty handed.

Sound like a Turkey

Unless you are lucky enough to be set up where gobblers happen to walk within range, you will have to use turkey calls to entice the turkeys to come to you. With male wild turkeys actively engaged in finding mates during spring, it is best to sound like a female turkey (or a group of female turkeys) looking for love.

There are various types of turkey calls on the market, each with its own benefits. Each type of call has its distinct sound, but the choice of call is really left to personal preference. Some calls, like friction (slate, glass, aluminum, etc.) calls, box calls, and push-button calls, are somewhat easier to use, but they require one or two hands to operate. Diaphragm calls, on the other hand, are hands-free. They consist of thin, wafer-like membranes that are placed in the hunter's mouth. When the hunter expels air and vocal vibrations over the diaphragm call, the call can be used to produce various hen turkey sounds. Instructions are included with most store-bought turkey calls, so novice users can practice before heading to the woods.

As mentioned earlier in this chapter, turkey hens will yelp, cluck, purr, cackle, cut, and putt depending on their

This 21-pound tom with a 10-inch beard finally came into range of my shotgun after more than an hour of calling.

communication needs and locations. Most experts will agree that the sound that attracts the most responses by gobblers is the yelp. The hen yelp, often referred to as the hen's mating call, consists of a string of repeating notes used to locate other turkeys. Learn to produce the hen yelp on your turkey call (or calls) by listening to actual turkeys in the woods or by listening to audio files that can be found on numerous web sites. Produce the yelp when you hear gobbles in the woods, and in most cases, the gobbler will respond with additional gobbles. Continue calling to entice the gobbler to come within shooting range. If you can see the gobbler, be careful not to let him see you calling. He will be looking for the hen that is making the sound, so the movement of your hands (if using a call other than a diaphragm call) may give you away.

In cases where stubborn gobblers are not fully committed to walking within range, try to attract the hens instead. If you can call hens toward you, the gobblers may follow. If the hens are making sounds, try to reproduce the sounds they are making. In many cases, the hens will become curious or angry and may walk to investigate your calls. Hopefully, a love-crazed gobbler will follow.

Although sounding like a hen can be effective, refrain from reproducing a putt call. A putt is generally an alarm call that alerts other turkeys to the presence of danger. In most cases when you hear a turkey putt, it is usually followed by the birds walking or running away from you.

Use Decoys

I have successfully hunted turkeys with and without using decoys, but I believe that the use of good decoys can give mature gobblers the added confidence and incentive to come within shooting range. When combined with good calling, turkey decoys can make the difference between a full pot and an empty bag.

Like goose and duck decoys, there are multiple types of turkey decoys on the market. There are shells, full bodies, inflatables, and even photograph-imprinted silhouettes. All of the decoys types can be effective, but there are a few things to consider.

Reflection

If you have ever seen a turkey in the sunlight, you know that its feathers have an iridescent, somewhat waxy-looking sheen. However, when using turkey decoys, it is important that they reflect or shine as little as possible.

Most turkey decoys give off some amount of light reflection, since they are usually made from plastic, vinyl, or foam, and they tend to even look a bit shinier when morning dew or frost forms on them. Be aware that mature turkeys may be apprehensive when they see sunlight sparkling off of a decoy. To minimize light reflections, carefully examine your decoys before purchasing them. If they appear too shiny under the lights of your hunting supply store, opt for a different brand or material; they will only shine more when sunlight hits them. Additionally, when hunting on days with little cloud cover, try to set up your decoys in shady locations where the sun will not hit them directly.

Movement

Turkey decoys can look more lifelike if they are able to move after being set up. Most turkey decoys, be they shells, full bodies, inflatables, or silhouettes, are anchored into the ground via plastic or metal stakes. In many instances, the stakes attach to the decoys in a manner that enables the decoy to move (wiggle or bob) with the wind. This little bit of

A bald eagle attacked this realistic looking hen decoy right after dawn. Notice the talon hole.

movement may be just enough to convince a wary gobbler to move a bit closer and into the range of your shotgun.

In addition to using the wind to slightly move turkey decoys, I have seen seasoned turkey hunters actually attach Canada goose wings to a turkey decoy and rig up a pulley system that causes the "turkey" wings to flap when a string is pulled. I have also seen turkey decoys attached to wire sleds that are pulled across the ground to mimic a walking turkey. These examples of ingenuity add more realism to the decoys and have led to the harvests of nice turkeys.

> Note: According to Delaware regulations, turkey decoys may have no parts from a formerly live turkey.[29]

During the spring 2010 turkey hunting season, I experienced how effective movement can be when applied to realistic looking decoys. I was turkey hunting a New Jersey public hunting area and used a photo-imprinted hen decoy. I set the lone decoy about fifteen yards into a plowed field, and I set up on the tree line of the field's edge. A slight wind was blowing the decoy, causing it to pivot on its metal stake.

Around 5:45 AM, I saw a bald eagle flying toward me. The eagle passed over me, and I lost sight of it. About thirty seconds later, the eagle swooped down and blasted my hen decoy! I heard the sound of wings, the sound of the bird crashing into the decoy, and the sound of the inflatable decoy popping. At first I thought someone shot the decoy, until I saw the eagle standing next to the deflated decoy dumbfounded. The eagle stood next to the decoy for about 30 seconds, then flew to a nearby tree and screeched for 30 minutes.

I am truly impressed with new technology used in decoy manufacturing. If that decoy fooled an eagle's eyes, it should work very well on wild turkeys.

Placement and Number of Decoys

Since your effective shooting range will probably not be more than about 40 yards, you should place your decoys within 10 to 25 yards of your shooting position, depending upon shooting angles, cover, terrain features, and turkey habits. Try to envision the angles at which turkeys will

---

[29] *Delaware Hunting & Trapping Guide*, 28.

12-year-old Coleby Etherton proudly displays a 5-beard, 21-pound gobbler harvested on a 2010 New Jersey youth hunt.

approach your decoys, and set up properly. After all, you want to drop a gobbler in his tracks – not blow your expensive decoys apart.

When using turkey decoys, I feel multiple decoys work better than one or two. Since turkeys usually live in flocks, I feel it looks more natural to a gobbler if he sees a group of decoys. Rather than one or two decoys, try setting out four, five, or more. Also, when using multiple decoys, it is a good idea to sound like multiple birds when you are calling. Be sure to know what flocks of feeding turkeys sound like, and use multiple calls, if needed, to produce different sounds.

Hen, Jake, or Gobbler Decoys?

Mature males turkeys will respond and react to turkey hen decoys as well as jake decoys. The big, bad gobblers out searching for a good time will approach hen decoys with hopes of getting lucky, but they will also aggressively (and sometimes violently) approach jake and even gobbler decoys in jealous rages to prevent the competition from scoring.

For safety reasons, I prefer to only use hen decoys, since, unfortunately, I have seen too many hunting safety videos of uneducated hunters targeting gobbler decoys. However, if you hunt on private land and are confident that no other hunters could possibly mistake your decoys for actual turkeys, jake and gobbler decoys could be your best bet. Many times when a dominant gobbler spots a jake or lesser gobbler with a hen, he comes running to chase the competitor away. In doing so, he is running directly toward the business end of your gun or bow. There are jake and gobbler decoys on the market that display the turkeys in full strut, half strut, and mating positions, and they can all be effective in luring a big tom into range.

Be Ready to Shoot

A common mistake made by turkey hunters is that they are not ready to shoot when a turkey comes within range. By being ready to shoot I mean literally having your gun shouldered and pointed toward the direction where you expect the turkey to present the best shot. In most cases, it is not enough to casually have your gun at your side, on the ground, or rested on your knees when the turkey is nearby. Once the turkey is close enough for you to shoot, he is close enough to see you move to grab your gun, shoulder it, and aim it (unless you are hunting from within an enclosed blind).

In situations where the turkey is close enough to see you but he is outside of your shooting range and not coming any closer, it is best to use a diaphragm call to try to draw him in. As mentioned earlier, using a friction call requires the use of your hands. Since any hand movement may spook the gobbler, keep your gun properly aimed and try calling with the diaphragm call. At that point, it is more important to remain still and not scare the turkey than it is to move and potentially ruin your hunt. If you cannot convince the turkey to come any closer, don't force it. Let him turn and walk away; you can then continue calling, reposition yourself, or let him go for another day.

In April 2010, a close friend wanted an introduction to turkey hunting and invited me on a Sussex County, Delaware turkey hunt. He is new to turkey hunting, so I jumped at the chance to provide some instruction to him while hopefully getting a chance at a gobbler myself.

We entered the woods around 5:10 AM and had just enough time to choose two trees, set up our decoys, and prepare for some action. Around 5:40 AM, I heard turkeys gobbling from their roosts. I figured we were about 200 yards from them, so I decided to move us closer. We quickly grabbed our guns (leaving the decoys and other gear behind), and moved about 100 yards closer to the gobbles.

I heard at least three separate birds gobbling, and I knew we would get some action. They were gobbling heavily until about 6:00 AM, then there was a pause for a few minutes. I figured the turkeys flew down from their roosts, so I told my friend to get ready to shoot. I began calling softly with slate and aluminum pot calls, and the birds were answering.

Within ten minutes, I knew at least one of the birds was moving toward us. I called a bit again, and he hammered back with a gobble. I heard his footsteps coming through the dry leaves and then saw his head rising over a small hill. He stopped about 45 yards away and fanned out. I could just barely see him, so I used my mouth call to call him again. He let out a thunderous gobble, and began walking up the path directly to us.

My buddy was about five yards from me, and I knew he saw the bird coming. I wasn't sure if he knew when to fire, so after waiting for what seemed like an eternity, I whispered, "SHOOT!" when the bird was about 15 yards away. He fired, but it looked like the first shot missed completely. He fired a second time. I saw some breast feathers rustle, then the big gobbler turned tail and ran away like a roadrunner being chased by a coyote.

Since my hunting partner was so close, I saw what went wrong. A common mistake, he was not truly ready to shoot. This was the first time he turkey hunted, and he was surprised by the gobbler's head coloration and constant head movement. He didn't get the gun fully shouldered and he didn't get his eye down on the sight. Instead he looked over the back sight of his shotgun, causing him to shoot low.

Wild Turkey Hunting

4

Small Game Hunting

Hunting small game is a big part of Delaware's hunting heritage. With many hunters getting their introductions to hunting by tagging along with Dad on squirrel and rabbit hunts, Delaware small game hunting is not only looked upon as a rite of passage for young hunters, it is also a time-honored tradition that enables hunters of all ages to commune with the past. Just like in centuries gone by, a small game hunter needs nothing more than a firearm of choice, a good pair of walking boots, and, perhaps, the instincts of a well-bred dog to fill his pot.

Small game species commonly hunted in Delaware include eastern gray squirrel, eastern cottontail rabbit, and bobwhite quail. Delaware also regulates hunting of ring-necked pheasants, raccoons, and possums, but the number of hunters who specifically target these species is relatively low. Prior to writing this chapter, I contemplated including information regarding pheasant hunting in Delaware. Granted, there are *some* wild ringnecks in Delaware, but in my years of small game hunting in Delaware with skilled bird dogs, I have encountered none. Therefore, I encourage each of you to be luckier than I am and bag a giant rooster, but I won't devote any more of this book to Delaware pheasant hunting. Likewise, I personally know several small game hunters who target raccoons and the occasional Virginia opossum. However, because of the relatively low number of hunters who participate in raccoon and possum hunts, I won't address them here.

Eastern Gray Squirrels

For those of you who are familiar with Delaware's wildlife, you already know about our squirrels. For those of you who are not, let me put it succinctly – squirrels are just about everywhere. Eastern gray squirrels, or just 'squirrels' as we Delawareans call them (although the more colorful name 'tree rats' comes to mind), are prolific and are found in New Castle, Kent, and Sussex Counties.

Note: The southern Delaware woods may also host a few Delmarva fox squirrels. Delmarva fox squirrels are listed as a threatened and endangered species and are longer, heavier, and paler than eastern gray squirrels. Be sure of your target before shooting. [30]

Habitat and Food

Squirrels nest and spend much of their time in the mature trees of forests and wooded plots where food sources are plentiful. Squirrels are omnivorous, with their diets consisting mostly of nuts, seeds, flowers, and buds, but, they will also eat fruits, plant bulbs, crops, and insects. To my surprise, I recently found out that squirrels may also eat their young, bird eggs and chicks, bones, and small amphibians, such as

---

[30] Coleman and Therres, Delmarva Fox Squirrel: Shore Lore & Legacy.

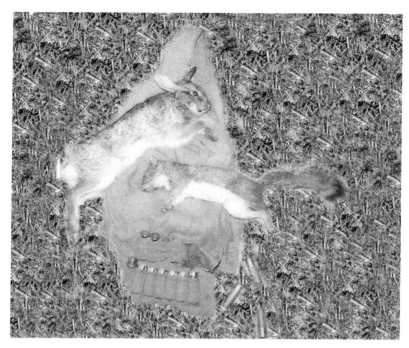

A typical Delaware small game harvest displays an eastern cottontail rabbit and an eastern gray squirrel.

frogs.[31] With Delaware's wooded areas ranging from expansive forests to backyard stands of oak and walnut trees, the state offers attractive habitat for squirrels.

If you ask any Delaware resident with a backyard bird feeder who lives near some mature trees, he will tell you that squirrels can be nuisances. They ravage accessible bird feeders by eating the birdseed and by gnawing down the wood. They dig up flower gardens to find bulbs. They find their ways in to garages, attics, and house walls. And, they

---

[31] University of Michigan Museum of Zoology Animal Diversity Web. *Sciurus carolinensis - eastern gray squirrel.*

can even cause blackouts for entire neighborhoods by shorting out power lines and transformers.

Since I am a Delaware resident who lives among trees, I can verify all of the aforementioned scenarios! Squirrels have ruined at least three of my birdfeeders by chewing through their support strings and causing them to crash to the ground. The squirrels then eat all of the spilled seed and chew through the wood to get at any remaining food. The squirrels are so crafty, in fact, that one got into my garage, climbed on some bicycles, jumped to the top of a sealed, plastic trash bin that was used for birdseed storage, and gnawed through the plastic spout of the container! Unfortunately for him, his plan didn't include a means of escaping the container. With my vizsla Gus going crazy, he managed to alert me that something was in the container. After realizing what was going on, I rescued the fattest squirrel I ever saw!

As further evidence that these critters can be nuisances, I now own a portable generator. One too many transformers have exploded near my home, and singed squirrel carcasses told me all I needed to know.

Delaware Squirrel Hunting Seasons and Methods

Delaware squirrel hunting seasons typically run for specified periods in the fall and winter, and are usually separated by Delaware firearm deer seasons. For example, the 2010-2011 Delaware gray squirrel season ran from September 15 through February 5, but it closed during the November shotgun deer season. Daily bag limits traditionally range from four to six squirrels, and legal hunting times are typically 30 minutes before sunrise to 30 minutes after sunset.

In specified seasons and in locations south of the Chesapeake and Delaware Canal, .22 caliber rimfire rifles can be used for squirrel.

In many parts of the country, squirrels are typically hunted with small-caliber rifles. In Delaware, regulations stipulate that squirrels may be hunted with shotguns throughout the state. Also, in locations south of the Chesapeake and Delaware Canal, .17 through .22 caliber rimfire and pellet rifles and muzzleloading rifles up to .36 caliber may be used.[32]

If you are hunting a heavily wooded area where you will have no long shots, I recommend using a 20-gauge or 12-gauge shotgun with a modified choke and an all-purpose field load of number 6 or 7 ½ shot. If you might have a chance at some longer shots (and you are hunting within Delaware's

---

[32] *Delaware Hunting & Trapping Guide*, 29.

legal areas), I recommend using a .22 rifle for plinking squirrels. The target practice and absence of pellets in the meat are both good reasons to opt for a .22.

For squirrel hunters looking for an added challenge, many try their hand at hunting squirrels with a bow. Range is much more limited and stealth and accuracy are key, but there are few things more satisfying to an archer than harvesting such a small, wary target. In fact, to tune up for big game hunting, some archers make it a point to hunt squirrels with a bow during the early parts of the season.

With the potential for Delaware regulations and seasons to change each year, be sure to thoroughly research and abide by all Delaware hunting laws and regulations as established in the annual *Delaware Hunting & Trapping Guide*.

Squirrel Hunting Hotspots

While many of us cannot hunt squirrels in our backyards (no matter how much we want to), there are a plethora of fine squirrel hunting locations in Delaware. As with all Delaware hunting, the hunter must consider whether he will hunt public or private land, but for the most part, there are few hunting locations where squirrels can't be found. Since good squirrel hunting locations are so numerous, it just doesn't make sense to attempt to mention all of the specific locations here. Instead, I will mention general areas on public hunting land where squirrel hunters can expect to have success.

One of the best ways to pinpoint top squirrel hunting hotspots on public hunting areas is to scout. If you are a deer and/or turkey hunter, look for squirrels and prime squirrel habitat while you are scouting for deer or turkey hunting. Look for prime food sources on the trees and on the ground, look for leafy squirrel nests in the crotches of trees, and listen for the chattering calls of squirrels. Quick walks through wooded areas on public hunting lands are sure to produce some good squirrel hunting locations.

When looking for squirrel hunting locations, consider the Warren/Faella Tract of the Augustine Wildlife Area in New Castle County, the Blackiston Wildlife Area in Kent County, and various tracts of Redden State Forest in Sussex County.

Techniques

Camouflage

Since most of the squirrels you will be hunting will be in the trees above you, there is a good chance they will see you on the ground. Therefore, proper camouflage is crucial for effective squirrel hunting.

It is important to match your camouflage patterns to the season you are hunting. It is also important to point out that the camouflage you would normally use for deer hunting may not be as effective against squirrels. In many cases, deer hunters hunt from elevated stands, so their camouflage clothing incorporates tree branches and leaves into their patterns. Since squirrels hunters typically hunt from the ground, it is more important to blend in with the forest floor and tree trunks, rather than tree branches and leaves. Most of the time, brown camouflage patterns are optimal. In addition to wearing camouflage clothing, covering up with camo netting or blankets is also helpful.

Stealth

With many of a squirrel's natural predators (including foxes, coyotes, cats, and raccoons) lurking on the ground, squirrels are extremely aware of any movement on the forest floor beneath them. Since a hunter with a rifle, shotgun, or bow is potentially more dangerous to a squirrel than any of its four-legged predators, it is rare for a squirrel not to notice a hunter walking through the woods. It is almost unavoidable to remain unnoticed while walking to a squirrel hunting location, but you can trick squirrels into thinking you left the area.

When walking into the woods to hunt squirrels, look for a good place to stop and set up on the ground. Find a location where you see signs of squirrels, find a comfortable spot on the ground, and sit. If the squirrels saw you walking in, chances are they will leave the area or hide until they feel it is safe to return or to show themselves. Therefore, it is important for you to remain as still and as quiet as possible until the squirrels show themselves.

When a squirrel presents itself and you have a safe, high-probability shot, slowly move to a firing position and shoot. Regardless of whether you hit the squirrel, it is usually a good practice to move locations after shooting. Squirrels will tend to scatter at the sound of close gunshots, and they may not return for lengthy periods of time.

Avoid Mid-Day Hunting

Because gray squirrels are most active in the 2-3 hours after sunrise and the 2-3 hours before sunset, it is most productive to hunt them in the early mornings and late afternoons. Although squirrels can be seen moving during the mid-day hours, it is more common for them to remain in their nests. Skilled squirrel hunters can coerce squirrels to show themselves by effectively using squirrel calls, but is advisable to avoid mid-day squirrel hunting.

Early Season vs. Late Season

I am frequently asked about the best time of year to hunt squirrels. Is it more productive to hunt squirrels early in the season or late in the season? As a true hunter who believes a bad day of hunting beats a good day at work every time, my answer is, "Hunt whenever you have the time." However, there are pros and cons associated with hunting earlier or later in the season.

As with most hunting, hunting early in the season gives the hunter the element of surprise. Mature squirrels have not seen hunters since the end of last year's season, and young squirrels may have never seen hunters. Additionally, the abundant foliage offers the hunter a bit more concealment when walking through the woods and when sitting on the ground. However, just as the foliage conceals the hunter, it also conceals the squirrels, making it more difficult to locate and shoot the animals.

Hunting squirrels late in the season can be good because it is much easier to see the squirrels. With most of the trees having lost their leaves, there is not much concealment for the squirrels. However, there is also little concealment for the hunter. Just as the hunter can easily see the squirrels, the squirrels can easily see the hunter. What's more, the squirrels may have experienced other hunters during the early parts of the season and may be more wary, making them tougher prey.

My personal preference is to hunt during the later parts of the season. Temperatures are lower, fewer bugs are around, and the critters are easier to see. Although the squirrels will be more wary, their instincts will still drive them to venture from their nests to collect food. Good camouflage, concealment, and stealth usually ensure an adequate harvest.

Retrieving Downed Squirrels

Here is an interesting tip that I learned from experience the first several times I squirrel hunted. I harvested my first few squirrels with a 12-gauge shotgun, and retrieved them relatively easily. However, there were some that I shot where I could not find them anywhere. I saw them drop from the trees to the ground, but cursory searches produced no results. I assumed that the squirrels were merely stunned and managed to escape after falling.

After discussing this with a fellow hunter, he offered me the advice that downed squirrels sometimes instinctively bury themselves in leaves before expiring. Thinking this could be the case, I went back to the spot where I lost a squirrel with my bird dog Gus. Sure enough, he found the downed squirrel about three inches under some dead leaves. I now make sure I always search through leaves when I cannot find a downed squirrel.

When retrieving squirrels, be absolutely certain they are dead before attempting to handle them. While targeting woodcocks and rabbits with Gus, a gray squirrel ran across my path. I shot the squirrel, and Gus instinctively went to retrieve him. The squirrel was not yet dead, and all hell broke loose! As Gus picked up the squirrel, the squirrel started screaming and bit into Gus' lip. Gus began to howl, ran around in circles, and kept trying to fling the squirrel off his lip much like a killer whale flings a seal through the air before killing it! Faced with two screaming animals, I had to grab the squirrel and pull him away from Gus, at which time the squirrel sank his claws into me before expiring.

Eastern Cottontail Rabbits

As with squirrels, eastern cottontail rabbits (or just 'rabbits' or 'cottontails' to Delawareans) are pervasive throughout Delaware's New Castle, Kent, and Sussex counties. Since a female rabbit can have about four or five babies three to four times a year, it is easy to see why rabbits are so widespread and are consequently among the most hunted animals in the United States.

Habitat and Food

Eastern cottontails are most often found in transitional areas between wooded tracts and open land, though they frequently feed in woods and fields. In Delaware, they can be found in thickets, hedgerows, phragmites stands, agricultural fields, marshes, meadows, pastures, backyards, and just about any other areas that provide them with adequate food and shelter.

Adult rabbits are solitary and usually establish home territories ranging from a few to more than 20 acres, but only females nest to bear and raise young. Female rabbits will dig small depressions for nests and line them with fur and soft foliage, but will only tend to the nest until the young leave (after about 2-3 weeks). Male and female rabbits (when not nesting) will rest and hide in places that offer them adequate camouflage and cover from predators and weather. Normally expect to find rabbits near fallen trees and in brush piles, under thick pine and cedar trees, among thorny bushes, and under old farm equipment. However, be aware that rabbits will also rest and take refuge in groundhog holes, under buildings structures (such as decks, barns, and sheds), and on islands created by incoming and outgoing tides.

Eastern cottontails are vegetarians, eating a variety of plants including grasses, clover, vegetables, fruit, grain, flowers, buds, branch tips, and bark. Rabbits prefer the lush, succulent food sources that are abundant in spring, summer, and early fall, but they will resort to eating twigs, bark, and other dried plant matter in late fall and winter. The cottontails are mostly nocturnal, but their feeding activity peaks 1-2 hours after dawn and just before to 1-2 hours after sunset.

Delaware Rabbit Hunting Season and Methods

Delaware rabbit hunting season typically begins in late fall (November) and ends in mid to late winter (late February), with daily bag limits traditionally set at four rabbits. Legal hunting times are typically 30 minutes before official sunrise to 30 minutes after official sunset.

Because of the small size and quick movements of eastern cottontails, I typically opt to hunt them with a 20-gauge, semi-automatic shotgun with an improved-cylinder choke and size 6 or 7 ½ high-velocity loads. I have effectively hunted rabbits with a 12-gauge, but the weight of the gun gets to be a burden on long hunts, and you tend to lose some meat on close shots. Also, I have used pump-action shotguns on rabbits, but because those cottontails move so quickly, I almost always use a semi-auto in case I need quick subsequent shots.

For a humbling experience, I recommend that archers try their hand at bowhunting rabbits. Unless you happen to sneak up on stationary rabbits, a compound bow is pretty ineffective while rabbit hunting because of the time needed to draw and aim at the target. If you are a traditional bow hunter and can shoot instinctively with a recurve or long bow, bowhunting for rabbits can be an exciting endeavor that will sharpen your skills.

Before hunting rabbits in Delaware, be sure to check all applicable Delaware hunting laws and regulations as established in the annual *Delaware Hunting & Trapping Guide*.

Rabbit Hunting Hotspots

Delaware rabbit harvests are not tracked like deer and turkey harvests, so it is difficult to pinpoint exact rabbit hunting hotspots. However, because rabbits are plentiful and can be found in most areas of the state, finding good rabbit hunting locations is not a problem.

As mentioned earlier, rabbits are one of the most commonly hunted game species in the United States, and as such, competition for good rabbit hunting locations is high. With many rabbit hunters and their dogs scouring the brush for rabbits on Delaware public hunting areas each season, it may be best to try to procure rights to hunt rabbits on private land. The prolific nature of rabbits can make them a nuisance to landowners because they eat crops and ornamental plantings. Therefore, many private landowners are receptive to hunters asking for permission to rabbit hunt their properties.

Three Delaware rabbits, harvested with a .410 and a 20-gauge.

If you cannot gain permission to hunt rabbits on private property, there are still plenty of rabbits to be had on Delaware public hunting lands. When looking for public land to hunt, consider locations that are off the beaten path. Most rabbit hunters will hit the easily accessible, high-profile public spots early and often, so just go elsewhere. Just like with squirrel hunting, use your deer and turkey scouting trips to also look for rabbits and signs of prime rabbit habitat. Record your scouting results in a notebook, and refer back to them when considering locations to rabbit hunt. Instead of going to the same old, common areas where you have traditionally seen rabbits and rabbit hunters, go to the spots you recorded in your scouting notebook. You know that most hunters will automatically go for hedgerows, thickets, and tall grass fields near the public parking areas, so plan to go deeper into the public areas. While most hunters are busy taking the "low hanging fruit" of the common areas, head toward the underbrush of marsh edges; phragmites patches along canals, rivers, and ponds; and old farmsteads where ramshackle equipment and buildings will harbor a multitude of cottontails. As an example of this practice, while deer and crow hunting public land along the Delaware River, I frequently saw rabbits dart across the trails that traversed through the stands of phragmites that lined the River. Recording this in my hunting notebook, I later suggested that we try rabbit hunting the same spot during the next year's rabbit season. We encountered no other hunters, and as it turned out, two hunting buddies and I all limited out on rabbits at that location.

After you determine some potential rabbit hotspots, I recommend using the 'hit and run' approach to rabbit hunting. Have several areas in mind where you want to hunt, and map a course so that you can get to them in successive fashion with as little travel time as possible. Quickly, but thoroughly, 'hit' the first spot by making a pass or two at the prime rabbit-hiding locations, and then pack up and 'run' to the next spot. Using the 'hit and run' approach not only enables you (and your dogs, if applicable) to cover more spots in a shorter amount of time, but you are also assured to not totally decimate any one location.

When looking for good rabbit hunting locations that receive relatively low hunting pressure, consider the Warren/Faella Tract of the Augustine Wildlife Area and the Chesapeake & Delaware Canal Wildlife Area in New Castle County, the Blackiston Wildlife Area in Kent County, and various tracts of Redden State Forest in Sussex County.

Techniques

Choose Hunting Times Wisely

As mentioned earlier, rabbits are mostly nocturnal, but their feeding activity peaks 1-2 hours after sunrise and just before to 1-2 hours after sunset. With this in mind, early morning or late-day hunts may be more productive than mid-day hunts, especially for rabbit hunters who are not using dogs. Since the rabbits are more apt to leave heavy cover in their searches for food, hunters without dogs can maximize their chances by scheduling their hunts in accordance with daylight rabbit feeding times.

However, since rabbit dogs will pick up the scents of rabbits that have been feeding earlier in the day, mid-day hunting can be an effective technique for rabbit hunters working with dogs. The dogs can follow the established scent trails and do the hard work of flushing the rabbits out of their mid-day hiding places, providing the hunters with quality shots. Additionally, since many hunters are finished their daily rabbit hunting by late morning, hunters with skilled dogs can hunt some of the same areas that were hunted

Frequently used for flushing out rabbits, beagles can also be taught to retrieve.

earlier in the day and achieve moderate success. Rabbits tend to stay in their home territories, and they sometimes circle back to the vicinities from which they were chased. After the morning hunters scare the rabbits into deep cover, the rabbits will usually be ready to scramble back toward their home turf. A team of hunters and dogs can easily flush the rabbits out after they have had a few hours to calm down.

Use the Weather to Your Advantage

Eastern cottontail rabbit fur does not have superior insulating qualities, and as such, the rabbits tend to shelter themselves from cold, wind, rain, and snow. Since rabbits are apt to hunker down during periods of inclement weather, a good technique is to hunt them immediately after bad weather passes. If a Delaware January ice storm brings two

113

days of clouds, rain, ice, and wind, plan to rabbit hunt the first sunny day after the storm subsides. The rabbits will leave shelter to find food and they will seek the warmth of open sunlight. Likewise, hunting rabbits after Delaware snow storms can be effective. One, rabbit tracks in the snow provide good indications of rabbit feeding and hiding places, and two, any flushed rabbits will be much easier to see against the white backdrop of fresh snow.

If you have the hankering to hunt during foul weather, do not fret—you too can find Delaware rabbits. Since the rabbits will attempt to shelter themselves from the weather, try to think like a cold, wet rabbit. Where would you go to escape the elements? That's right, you would go under a thick pine or cedar tree, beneath the branches and leaves of a fallen oak, in a thick tangle of brush, or under the farmer's rusted, old tractor. Go to these sheltered areas with dogs or without, and you will inevitably flush out some cottontails.

Hunt with Two or More People

Whether hunting rabbits with dogs or without, you will be sure to increase your harvest rate by hunting with a partner or two. It never fails that at least once a hunt a rabbit flushes on the exact opposite side of the brush pile you are kicking and presents you with no shot. As the rabbit runs away snickering, you wish you had a buddy set up on the other side of the brush pile.

To maximize your chances of success, take the team approach to rabbit hunting. Each member of the hunting party can walk together at set distances apart from each other, and you can take turns kicking and stomping potential rabbit hiding spots. If each member is situated properly, someone should get a shot if a rabbit flushes.

Another effective method is to set a hunter (or group of hunters) at a strategic location near a natural funnel where rabbits are apt to run if pressured. A second group of hunters and/or dogs walks or 'pushes' the areas leading to the funnel with hopes that any flushed rabbits will run to the location where the first group is waiting.

Dress Appropriately

It is not necessary to wear camouflage when rabbit hunting, but it is advisable to wear clothing that will protect you from thorns, burrs, jagged branches, ticks, and sprained ankles. Since we hunters are each around 6 feet tall, give or take a few inches, we are at an extreme disadvantage when trying to walk through the same habitat where 6- to 10-inch tall rabbits run at speeds up to 15 miles an hour. While the rabbits go *under* all of the hazards, we pretty much have to go *through* them.

When gearing up for rabbit hunting, consider heavy brush pants or heavy hunting chaps that pull over your boots and jeans. Wear long sleeve coats made of material that will not have a tendency to get hung up in thorns, and wear sturdy boots that provide adequate protection against ankle sprains, but that also are light enough to walk long distances. I also recommend wearing a hat and gloves to protect your head and hands from bugs, thorns, and poison ivy. It is also important to note that Delaware rabbit hunters are required to wear at least 400 square inches of hunter orange on their chest, back, and head when hunting during any deer firearm

Dress appropriately for rabbit hunting. Consider wearing heavy brush pants or hunting chaps, durable coats, sturdy boots, and hunter orange.

season.[33] A hunter orange vest and hat typically satisfy this requirement, but I suggest wearing the orange during all of

---

[33] *Delaware Hunting & Trapping Guide*, 29.

your rabbit hunts. Rabbit cover can be pretty darn thick and difficult to see through, so wearing hunter orange is a potential safeguard against any misplaced shots.

Practice Shooting at Rabbit-Like Targets

Shooting a running rabbit can be a difficult task to those who are unfamiliar with shooting downward at moving targets. Eastern cottontails can leap distances up to 15 feet, and they typically run in zigzag fashion making it challenging to hit them with fatal shots.

Most of us are accustomed to shooting clay pigeons in flight as practice for migratory bird and waterfowl hunting, but few of us actually practice at shooting targets on the ground. To practice for rabbit hunting, there is nothing better than participating in some sporting clays shoots where the courses incorporate targets that are rolled and bounced along the ground. The erratic nature of the rolling targets mimics the actions of a flushed rabbit, and practicing shooting the targets will lead to greater success in the field.

Bobwhite Quail

Many hunters will tell you that the quail population in Delaware and across the United States has declined significantly over the past 30 years, but there are still some coveys of wild bobwhite quail to be found in The First State. Unlike my encounters (or lack thereof) with wild pheasants in Delaware, I have personally encountered and harvested Delaware wild bobwhite quail.

I frequently mention "wild" quail or pheasants so that I can make the distinction between the pen-raised and released birds that are hunted on public and private game farms.

Oftentimes these released birds escape the game farms unharmed and take up residence in close proximity to their release locations. In most cases, none of the pen-raised birds survive in the wild for very long, but it is possible to encounter them while hunting. I can usually tell the difference between wild and pen-raised birds because the pen-raised birds are huge in comparison to their wild counterparts. Likewise, wild quail tend to flush and fly quickly when hunted, while many pen-raised birds are content to sit on the ground in front of you or just walk away.

Habitat and Food

Delaware bobwhite quail can be found in many of the same areas that Delaware rabbits inhabit. Quail are primarily ground dwelling birds, so they nest, sleep, and eat on the ground (although they occasionally roost on the branches of low trees and bushes). Therefore, like rabbits, quail are most often found in transitional areas between wooded tracts and open fields, where thick woodland edges provide adequate cover from predators.

In Delaware, expect to find quail in dense thickets, hedgerows, fencerows, and forest edges that border open fields. To increase your chances of success in finding Delaware quail, look for the aforementioned locations in areas of early successional growth, which is ground that has been burned or plowed in the last three years. The new (successional) vegetation that appears during this period satisfies the food and shelter needs of quail quite well.[34] In fact, in speaking with several Delaware quail hunting old timers and heavily researching this issue, it is evident that

---

[34] *Bobwhite Basics.*

many believe the decline in the quail population is due to the new, 'clean-farming' methods where "double cropping, fall plowing, increased herbicide and insecticide use, mowing idle lands, removal of fence rows, and cropping that extends to the extreme edge of fields"[35] are eliminating much of the prime quail habitat and food sources. Therefore, locating areas that are conducive to sustaining quail populations is crucial to successful hunts.

Depending upon seasonal availability, quail eat seeds, mast, and crops, but they also feed on insects and the leaves of young vegetation. In Delaware, prime food sources for quail include grass seeds, ragweed seeds, acorns, sweet gum seeds, and even poison ivy berries. They also are attracted to Delaware's soybeans, wheat, millet, sorghum, and corn, so search for hunting locations near Delaware agricultural fields, if possible.

With the exception of breeding season, quail live in coveys (groups) of five to more than twenty-five birds and roam areas of twenty to forty acres.[36] The coveys provide quail with protection, since each member of the group can be on the lookup for predators. If a predator threatens the covey, all of the birds will flush (fly) at once, startling and confusing the predator.[37] Additionally (and similar to some penguins in this regard), the covey also provides warmth during winter. While on the ground, the quail back themselves together in concentric circles (commonly referred to as 'pie-plating') so that the innermost birds are sheltered from any cold and

---

[35] Fred Ward, Rick Chastain, Eddie Linebarger, David Long, Kenny Vernon, Rick Fowler, Brian Infield, and Randy Guthrie, *Strategic Quail Management Plan.*

[36] *Bobwhite Basics.*

[37] *Bobwhite Basics.*

wind. Each of the birds alternates its position so that time is spent in the warmer and colder parts of the circles. A good method for locating quail is to look for droppings from multiple birds arranged in a circular, pie-plate-like fashion on the ground. If you find such concentrations of droppings in fields or under bushes, you can conclude that quail are nearby.

Delaware Quail Hunting Season and Methods

Delaware bobwhite quail hunting season usually runs in parallel to rabbit season, typically beginning in late fall (November) and ending in mid-winter (January or February). Daily bag limits are traditionally set at six birds, and legal hunting times are typically 30 minutes before official sunrise to 30 minutes after official sunset.

As with hunting rabbits and squirrels, Delaware regulations stipulate that quail may be hunted with shotguns 10 gauge or smaller. Quail are among the smallest of game birds, and they usually fly fast and low to the ground. With these facts in mind, I usually hunt quail with a 20-gauge, semi-automatic shotgun with an improved-cylinder choke and size 7 ½ high-velocity loads. Much of the shooting at flushed quail will be extremely fast, so lightweight guns with shorter barrels (for maneuvering and aiming through trees and brush) are more desirable. Likewise, the speed of a semi-auto may be needed, one, because you may have shots at multiple birds in the covey, and two, quail can be tough to hit.

Remember, before hunting quail in Delaware, be sure to check all applicable Delaware hunting laws and regulations as established in the annual *Delaware Hunting & Trapping Guide*.

Quail Hunting Hotspots

My trusted Hungarian vizsla Starr Point's Gustav of Glenside JH (aka "Gus"), a few hunting partners, and I have traversed Delaware's public and private lands in search of bobwhite quail. To my delight (and surprise), we have located quail in all three counties. I have only hunted and harvested quail in New Castle and Kent counties, but, believe it or not, I have seen and heard bobwhites while crossing dunes to surf fish on Delaware beaches.

Without a doubt, successfully locating and harvesting Delaware quail is much simpler with a good bird dog, and I am hesitant to recommend that any hunter pursue quail without at least one dog. My vizsla Gus has found and pointed entire coveys of quail while we were quail hunting, and he has found and pointed single quail while we were woodcock hunting. In just about every case, I am convinced that we would have never even located the birds without the dog. However, there are methods that can increase your chances of success when hunting without a dog. Read the *Techniques* section below for tips that can help hunters who wish to harvest Delaware quail without a dog.

Although they prefer similar habitat, quail are not as easy to find as rabbits. As stated earlier, you will probably have more success if you focus your efforts on hunting the hedgerows, fencerows, and forest edges that include early successional growth. Whether hunting private or public land, try to find locations that border crop fields whose farming methods support quail habitat and food sources.

Author's vizsla Gus points a single quail in a row of standing sorghum.

Do not discount or overlook Delaware's public hunting areas when building your quail hunting plans. Some Delaware public hunting areas are specifically managed for quail, and many of the public hunting areas include agricultural fields bordered by woods, tree lines, and brush lines. When seeking prime quail hunting locations on Delaware public land, consider the Chesapeake & Delaware Canal Wildlife Area and the Augustine Wildlife Area in New Castle County, the Blackiston Wildlife Area in Kent County, and Delaware Seashore State Park in Sussex County. I have successfully hunted quail at the Canal, Augustine, and Blackiston areas, and I have seen coveys of quail at Delaware Seashore State Park. In fact, Blackiston Wildlife Area includes several agricultural fields, sunflower fields, and other strip-crop type fields that provide phenomenal habitat and food for quail.

Techniques

Listen for Quail before Dawn

Those hunters who subscribe to the "the early bird gets the worm" school of thought know from experience that quail call excitedly at dawn. If hunters arrive near suspected quail roosts before dawn, they can pinpoint covey locations with some degree of accuracy if they hear their calls. A study conducted by D. Clay Sisson and H. Lee Stribling of the Auburn University Department of Zoology/Wildlife Science confirms this belief. They found that quail covey calls are intense just at daylight, but they are short-lived. According to their findings:

> "At 06:30 birds were inactive and woods were quiet. At 06:35 chaos broke loose, and quail were calling from what seemed like everywhere. By 06:40 the calling had stopped."[38]

They further describe that another, less-intense calling period occurs just before dark, but few calls are heard during the rest of the day.

For all quail hunters, but especially for those without the aid of bird dogs, using this knowledge to locate birds is invaluable. Arriving an hour or two earlier can save three or four hours of walking and searching for quail. When arriving at your hunting spot in the pre-dawn hours to locate quail, listen for their distinctive, high-pitched *bob-white* or *bob-bob-white* whistle. If you hear nothing, it could mean that there are

---

[38] D. Clay Sisson and H. Lee Stribling, Patterns of Bobwhite Covey Activity.

no quail near the location, but (since you are there) you might as well hunt it anyway. As an alternative to arriving earlier on your hunt days, you can always scout areas before you actually hunt them. Go to some potential locations before work or church (since you cannot hunt on Sunday in Delaware), and listen for quail calls at dawn. Likewise, as with turkeys, scout the night before a hunt. If you hear quail calling from a location just before dark, there is a good chance they will be at or near the same location in the morning.

Use the Weather to Your Advantage

A little research really does go along way. As a quail hunter, I have just taken certain tidbits of information for granted, and never really considered their origin, legitimacy, or efficacy. Just from hearing things that have been passed down for generations by other hunters and through my own experiences, I know that weather affects game in different ways. However, it was not until I actually read the previously mentioned report from Sisson and Stribling that I realized there are hard facts that support my beliefs about hunting and weather.

In their study of quail covey activity, Sisson and Stribling found that high quail activity occurred in cold weather, high relative humidity, and light winds; and lower quail activity levels occurred during hot weather, low humidity, rain, and strong winds, especially in winds blowing from the east.[39] Although good dogs can locate quail in most weather conditions, your chances of hunting success should be increased if you hunt on days that point to high quail activity levels.

---

[39] D. Clay Sisson and H. Lee Stribling, Patterns of Bobwhite Covey Activity.

Additionally, as with many types of game, it seems that quail can sense weather changes. In their study, Sisson and Stribling found that quail activity increased the day before an approaching weather front, so it may be best for hunters to monitor weather forecasts. If windy, wet weather is predicted, hunt the day before the foul weather is supposed to arrive. In anticipation of the front, the quail should be actively searching for food, since they may be forced to take shelter during the period of inclement weather.

Dress Appropriately

As I began writing this section, I realized that my clothing guidelines for quail hunting are just about identical to my guidelines for rabbit hunting. Therefore, rather than boring you with the same information, I will ask you to refer back to the *Dress Appropriately* information in the *Eastern Cottontail Rabbit* section of this chapter.

Shoot Safely

Quail are unlike a lot of game birds in that they flush in groups of birds that fly in all directions, fast and low to the ground. Because the birds fly low in comparison to most other game birds, it is of utmost importance to consider safety before squeezing the trigger.

As evidenced by the unfortunate incident involving Vice President Dick Cheney in February 2006 where he inadvertently shot a hunting companion while quail hunting, accidents do happen. Because thick brush, tall grass, cornstalks, bushes, and trees can obscure your vision when shooting at low-flying quail, always be sure you have a safe

Steven Kendus' vizsla Gus (wearing blaze orange) and Steven Kendus (wearing blaze orange cap, blaze orange and brown brush shirt, hunting chaps over jeans, and sturdy, lightweight boots) prepare to hunt quail on Blackiston Wildlife Area.

shot before firing. Watch out for humans and hunting dogs, and be aware of any obstacles that could cause ricochets.

Delaware quail hunters are required to wear at least 400 square inches of hunter orange on their chest, back, and head when hunting during any deer firearm season.[40] A hunter orange vest and hat typically satisfy this requirement, but, as with rabbit hunting, I suggest wearing orange during all of your quail hunts so that other hunters can see you more easily.

Predators

Some would argue that predator hunting should not be classified as small game hunting, but since it is a relatively new concept to Delaware hunters, we will address it in this chapter. Increasing numbers of foxes and coyotes are making their homes in Delaware's backyards, fields, forests, and marshes, so it's only a matter of time before more Delaware hunters begin targeting these species.

Red Foxes

Most Delaware hunters and farmers have encountered red foxes in the woods and fields, but the sly and intelligent red fox can be found in all areas of the state. I have seen red foxes in my yard, on the beach and boardwalk, on the highway, on city streets, near pond edges, and on school playgrounds, so it is easy to see that their population is booming.

---

[40] *Delaware Hunting & Trapping Guide*, 29.

Adaptable and opportunistic, expect to find red foxes in just about any type of environment – urban, suburban, or rural.

Habitat and Food

Red foxes are adaptable and opportunistic. Found throughout North America, Europe, Asia, and northern Africa, their habitat varies greatly. In Delaware, expect to find red foxes in New Castle, Kent, and Sussex counties in just about any type of environment – urban, suburban, or rural – where food sources are abundant.

Red foxes are primarily nocturnal, although it is not rare to see them during daylight hours. Red foxes stalk and hunt small birds and mammals (including mice, voles, squirrels, rabbits, cats, and groundhogs), but they also eat readily available food, such as pet food, vegetables, fruit, berries, insects, worms, frogs, and fish.

Red foxes typically hunt alone, but I have personally witnessed two foxes jointly hunting a house cat. Around 4:00 AM one winter night I was awakened by the high-pitch yelps of a fox and the crazed barks of my dog Gus. With Gus pawing at the front door to get out, I looked out the window and saw two red foxes circling a neighborhood house cat seeking refuge under my truck. Not thinking too clearly in my barely awake 4:00 AM stupor, I opened the door to get a better view. Gus bolted out barking like mad, and all hell broke loose! Both foxes began yelping, the cat coiled back and hissed, and Gus (since his instinct is to point game) locked up on point on three different scents.

The eyes of the foxes and the cat were all fixed on Gus. Seeing a chance for escape, the cat began to bolt. To my surprise, Gus went directly after the cat, and the foxes scattered. With Gus stopped in his tracks by my invisible dog fence, the cat was able to make a successful getaway (although I think the ruckus woke half the neighborhood).

Physical Characteristics

Red foxes get their names from their predominantly red coats, but red foxes can actually be any combination of red, brown, gray, black, white, silver, and gold. Their feet, lower legs, and backs of ears are usually black, and almost all red foxes have white-tipped tails.[41]

Similar in size to a small dog, adult red foxes are usually between 15 and 18 inches tall, about three feet long, and

---

[41] eNature.com. *Red Fox.*

weigh between 7 and 15 pounds. They have superb senses of smell and hearing, which they use to their advantage for finding prey.

Red foxes typically sleep outside of dens, using their thick fur and bushy tails to blankets themselves. Female red foxes will birth and rear young in dens, potentially giving birth to a litter of two to twelve kits.[42]

From experience, I can tell you that Delaware red foxes are quite vocal. Like dogs, red foxes have multiple barks, cries, yelps, squeals, and howls. On multiple occasions (including my dog, cat, and fox encounter mentioned above) I have seen and heard foxes yelping or barking, for lack of better descriptions. Many red fox sounds can easily be confused with those from a house pet, but red foxes make an easily discernable drawn-out cry. To give you an idea of what this fox cry sounds like, consider the high-pitched barks a little, yappy lapdog makes, then expand its individual bark by about a second. Instead of the lapdog's high-pitched, *yap yap yap yap* in quick succession, a red fox's cry is a more raspy *yaaaaaaaaaap, yaaaaaaaaaap, yaaaaaaaaaap* sound. I have seen foxes directly in front of me make this call, and it is an unmistakable and eerie sound.

Delaware Red Fox Hunting Season

Delaware has traditionally allowed red fox trapping (by licensed trappers) and red fox chases (on private land only), but 2010 marked the first time in recent history where a true red fox hunting season was implemented in Delaware.

According to the 2010-2011 *Delaware Hunting & Trapping Guide*:

---

[42] animals.nationalgeographic.com. *Red Fox.*

Red fox may be killed in accordance with the statutes and regulations of the State of Delaware governing the hunting of red fox from November 1 through the last day of February, excluding Sundays. It is unlawful to kill a red fox that is being pursued by dogs. Red foxes may be killed using a longbow, crossbow, shotgun, rimfire or center fire rifle up to .25 caliber or a muzzle-loading rifle. During any deer firearms season, it will be unlawful to hunt red fox with any firearm that is not also legal for deer hunting.

Legal hunting times are typically 30 minutes before official sunrise to 30 minutes after official sunset.

Techniques

In discussions with Delaware deer hunters, it seems that shooting foxes has been mainly an opportunistic endeavor. On properties where landowners were issued special fox control permits, hunters tell me that the landowners asked them to shoot any foxes they see. Therefore, most fox hunting in Delaware has really only been shooting of foxes that happen to cross paths of hunters pursuing other game.

With the implementation of the true red fox hunting season in 2010, hunters may actually try to employ some strategy when pursuing foxes.

Use Animal Distress Call to Lure Them In

The sensitive ears of red foxes are always listening for the sounds of their prey with hopes a quick meal is close by. A good way to get a shot at a nice red fox is to use this predatory instinct to bring him within range of your gun.

For those of you who have heard wounded or struggling rabbits, birds, or squirrels, you know the commotion their high-pitched squeals, squawks, and hisses make. These sounds are great lures for red foxes.

Mimicking the distress calls of red fox prey is fairly simple. Predator hunting mouth and hand calls are readily available at hunting supply stores, and they are easy to use. Some basic practice gives you the ability to makes squeals, squeaks, screams, and howls. Use loud calling to grab a fox's attention, but soften the calls as you see him approach.

For ease of use and added realism, consider purchasing an automatic caller for red fox hunting. Typically the same automatic caller can be used for crows and snow geese, so they are a good investment for the all-around hunter. Remote-controlled automatic callers with adjustable-volume speakers are your best bet. There are many callers on the market with a wide variety of predator hunting sounds available for the callers. Typical distress sounds include recordings from rabbits, chickens, fawns, mice, woodpeckers, and turkeys, but be sure to use sounds of animals that frequent the area your are hunting.

Find Them First

As with most hunting, it helps if you know where the game is likely to be before you head to the woods and fields. Red fox hunting is no exception. Although red foxes are found throughout Delaware, you can definitely maximize your odds if you are one hundred percent sure a fox is within range of your calls.

Foxes like to hunt in the early morning and late afternoon/early evening hours when prey is active, and they like to sleep in sunny, wind-protected locations during the day. Therefore, when seeking a red fox hunting location, try to locate a fox before you begin calling. Walk around field edges, observe abandoned farm buildings, or walk well-used game trails to find moving foxes, sleeping foxes, or fresh tracks.

We all know that foxes are sly and skittish, so be careful when trying to spot and stalk foxes. However, it is possible to walk within calling and shooting range of them. While crow hunting along the banks of the Delaware River, I saw a red fox curled up sleeping on the sun-drenched top of the bank. I was able to walk within 20 feet of him before he even knew I was there. If I was actually hunting this fox, I probably wouldn't have risked walking that close. Instead, I would have set up about 100 yards from him and tried to call him to me, but the fact still remains that I could have easily had the fox in my bag.

Coyotes

Although many Delaware residents find it hard to believe, it is absolutely true that coyotes inhabit all three Delaware counties, and their numbers may be on the rise. According to Joe Rogerson, game mammal biologist for the Delaware Division of Fish and Wildlife, Delaware has seen a gradual increase in reported coyote sightings since 2000.

With coyotes (and coyote hunting seasons) in Pennsylvania, New Jersey, and Maryland, it was only a matter of time before they migrated to Delaware's fields and marshes. I have heard about coyote sightings in Delaware since the early 1990s, and I know an injured coyote was captured near the Delaware Memorial Bridge around 2004. However, I now have absolute proof that coyotes inhabit Delaware.

34-pound female coyote harvested by John Massey with a bow near Middletown, Delaware in 2009.

In September 2008, Delaware hunter John Massey was deer hunting the edge of a cornfield and witnessed a large coyote walk passed his stand at 20 yards. Later that evening, John shot a deer. While dragging the deer out of the field, he heard corn crunching and noticed the shape of the coyote several rows into the corn. Shadowing John's every move, the coyote snarled, snorted, and barked at John and stayed with him step for step for 200 yards. When John reached the edge of the cornfield, the coyote trotted away.

In November 2009, John hunted the same location and again saw a coyote. This time the hunt ended differently. The coyote stopped 20 yards from him, and John launched an arrow that dropped the 34-pound female coyote in its tracks.

In addition to the coyote mentioned above, several other Delaware coyotes were harvested by hunters and trappers recently, while others fell victim to automobiles.

Habitat and Food

Although coyotes can be found in Delaware's wooded areas, they typically prefer fields and low brushy areas. They sleep and give birth in dens that they will dig themselves or take over from groundhogs.

Coyotes are opportunistic hunters and feeders and will eat just about anything, including carrion, small mammals, rodents, reptiles, amphibians and birds. They also eat insects, fruits, vegetables, livestock, pets, pet food and garbage.

Physical Characteristics

About the size of small collie or German shepherd, the coloration of coyotes varies. Coyotes are typically multi-colored with fur that contains gray, brown, red, white, black, and blond.

Coyotes are typically 30–34 inches long with a 12–16 inch tail, stand 23–26 inches tall, and weigh from 15–45 pounds. Breeding from late January through March, coyotes have an average of 6 pups, though litters can contain as many as 19 pups. [43]

Delaware Coyote Hunting Season

As of 2010, Delaware does not list the coyote as a game species and consequently does not have a coyote hunting season.

---

[43] Wikipedia. *Coyote.*

As hunters and trappers encounter coyotes more frequently, Delaware officials are considering listing coyotes as a game species. The current laws are open to interpretation, since some people believe that not being listed as a game species means coyotes are protected, while others feel that not being listed means they are unprotected.

Although creating a coyote hunting season would require State legislation, I feel a hunting season may come soon. Increasing numbers of coyote sightings combined with coyote reproduction rates should create a population that supports coyote hunting.

5

Migratory Bird Hunting

To many Delaware hunters there is nothing more pleasing than spending fall and winter days pursuing doves, woodcocks, and crows that use Delaware's fields, forests, and marshes as stopping points on their migratory journeys. Although some doves, woodcocks, and crows live in Delaware year round, others migrate through the State and are therefore classified as migratory birds, along with snipes, moorhens, gallinules, and various species of rails.

All migratory birds are protected by federal law, so hunting seasons, bag limits, and possession limits are set in accordance with United States Fish and Wildlife Service guidelines.

Mourning Doves

Typically regarded as the unofficial opening of the hunting season, dove hunting is enjoyed by Delaware hunters in New Castle, Kent, and Sussex Counties. With mourning doves plentiful throughout Delaware, many hunters take to the field each September with hopes of harvesting these tasty, yet challenging, birds.

Habitat and Food

Recognized as the most widespread game bird in North America, mourning doves (or just 'doves' to Delawareans) are just about everywhere in Delaware. They inhabit urban, suburban, and rural areas, and can be found nesting, feeding, or roosting near woods, farms, backyards, and city buildings. Doves usually mate for life and normally nest in trees, both deciduous and coniferous.

Doves eat seeds almost exclusively, but they will occasionally eat invertebrates, such as insects and snails. While they seem to prefer some types of seeds over others, doves usually eat the wild seeds of grasses, sweet gum, and smartweed in Delaware. Additionally, they are frequently found eating seed from bird feeders (including millet, safflower, and sunflower seeds) and agricultural crops, such as corn, soybeans, wheat, and sorghum. Delaware doves are so attracted to sunflower seeds, in fact, that the Delaware Division of Fish and Wildlife plants sunflower fields at specific public hunting areas and designates the fields as dove hunting areas. Like many birds, doves need to ingest gravel or 'grit' to aid digestion. After feeding, doves can be found on dirt roads, sand pits, stream banks, and parking lots hunting and pecking for bits of grit.

When considering locations for hunting doves, do a little research and scouting. As always, try to combine multiple scouting trips into one. While you are out on a walk through the woods, bring a notebook and note when and where you see or hear doves (or any other game you intend to hunt).

Look for doves feeding in fields, pecking gravel on cleared areas or beside roads, or perching on telephone wires and dead trees. After finding good concentrations of doves, visit the place several times and plan to stay for a while each time. Observe the doves and try to pattern their movements. Watch which ways they fly, where they land, and what times they move. If the doves tend to do the same things at the same times on multiple days, you can assume that they have a daily pattern that you can use to plan your hunts.

Delaware Dove Hunting Season

The Delaware mourning dove hunting season is typically broken up into multiple segments. For example, the 2010-2011 dove season ran for approximately four weeks in September, approximately two weeks in October, and approximately four weeks extending from mid-December to mid-January. In previous years, the first segment of the Delaware dove season stipulated that dove could only be hunted from noon to official sunset, but recent regulatory changes (beginning with the 2007-2008 seasons) set the legal hunting hours for all segments at 30 minutes before official sunrise to official sunset. Daily bag limits are usually 12-15 birds.[44]

In addition to normal licensing requirements, all Delaware dove hunters must register with the Federal Harvest Information Program (H.I.P.) so that the Delaware Division of Fish & Wildlife and the United States Fish and Wildlife Service can develop reliable estimates of the number of doves harvested. The estimates enable biologists to make sound decisions concerning dove population management, hunting seasons, and bag limits.

---

[44] *Delaware Hunting & Trapping Guide*, 29.

Delaware regulations stipulate that doves may be hunted with shotguns 10-gauge or smaller. Doves, which can fly at speeds up to 55 mph[45], can fly high and erratically. Because these aerobatic dare devils fly high and can change direction so quickly, they make for extremely challenging shooting. When I am mostly interested in harvesting doves for the pot, I usually hunt dove with a 12-gauge, semi-automatic shotgun with an improved-cylinder choke and size 7 ½ high-velocity loads. I figure the 12-gauge gives me the extra distance, if needed. If I want a more challenging experience, I will bring out the 20-gauge with a similar configuration and loads. But guys who are much better shots than I, enjoy hunting doves with .410.

Whichever gun you plan to use for dove hunting, make sure you bring enough shells! The experts say that two doves for every five shots is good, so if you plan on harvesting your limit, that means you should have at least 30 shells (assuming you're an expert). For the rest of us, plan on bringing two boxes of shells, plus another box for backup!

Recent Delaware regulations have stipulated that all hunters must use non-toxic shot when dove hunting on Delaware State Wildlife Areas during the month of September. Therefore, before hunting doves in Delaware, be sure to check all applicable Delaware hunting laws and regulations as established in the annual *Delaware Hunting & Trapping Guide*.

Dove Hunting Hotspots

When attempting to compile a list of dove hunting hotspots, I realized that there are just too many to list. Doves

---

[45]Wikipedia. *Mourning Dove.*

can be found all over Delaware, so any amount of scouting can quickly and easily locate birds.

Although doves can probably be found on almost every Delaware public hunting area, consider hunting those public locations that are specifically managed for doves. Some public hunting areas that include managed dove fields are: the Silver Run tract of the Augustine Wildlife Area in New Castle County; Blackiston and Milford Neck Wildlife Areas in Kent County; and the Muddy Neck Tract of Assawoman Wildlife Area in Sussex County. Be aware that some public hunting areas have specific regulations for dove hunting.

Techniques

Hunt Near Food and/or Water Sources

Doves usually feed early in the day, so they will leave their roosts in the morning in search of feeding areas. If you have done your homework and you have patterned some doves, you will be able to predict where they will feed. Set up in a tree line on the edge of a field where the doves will feed, and wait them out. If their established patterns hold true, they should arrive around the same times each day. Be sure to set up in a location where you will be presented with good shots as the doves fly to or from the field. Keep in mind their flight angles, and try to set up where the birds will be swooping down or taking flight so that they are within effective range.

Similar to hunting near food sources, hunting water sources can be effective. After completing your morning hunt, head back to the truck, have lunch, and take a nap. In the late afternoon hours, head back out to the field and set up near a body of water. After feeding, doves often head toward water

Two mid-season limits of mourning doves show a good day's hunt.

to drink before they head back to their roosts. Again, if you have properly patterned the doves, you will know which watering holes they will head to. Set up in a tree line, phragmites, or other cover near the water source before any doves begin to arrive. The birds will normally show up about an hour or two before dusk, but they may be there earlier, especially if their feeding areas are nearby or if the weather has been dry.

Camouflage

Unless you like shooting at dipping, diving, dancing, and flaring targets, be sure to use effective camouflage when dove hunting. Like waterfowl and crows, high-flying doves are able to see flashy objects, strange silhouettes, and stark color variations, and they will not fly by or land near things that make them uneasy.

Like turkey and deer hunting, it is imperative that dove hunters match their camouflage to the surroundings of their hunting spots and modify it according to the changing seasons. Early season dove hunts will call for bright green camo, while mid- and late-season hunts demand camo patterns that include more browns and grays. Be sure to cover your face with a mask or net, and be sure your hands are covered with gloves. As doves fly in and you begin to shoulder your gun for a shot, the slight movement combined with the potentially bright color or flash of skin can be enough to cause the birds to flare and head elsewhere.

Be Still

As mentioned above, doves can pick up the slightest unexpected movement as they are flying toward you. With this in mind, it is imperative to be as still as possible for as long as possible until a high-probability shot presents itself. We instinctively want to shoulder our guns as soon as doves begin to come in range, but in most cases, the doves will see us move and will flare away. Likewise, we are curious creatures, and we want to swivel our heads around to look at other birds coming in. In most cases, the doves will see this movement as well, and they will probably laugh at us as they sail out of range.

To give yourself the best chance of harvesting good numbers of doves, get situated in a comfortable shooting position and stay put. If needed, bring a camouflage, low-glare stool, chair, or bucket with you to your dove hunting location and set it up in an optimal shooting location. Keep your gun in hand so that you can shoulder it quickly with as little movement as possible. Alternatively, you can hunt doves from a blind, so that your movements are shielded from view. In this scenario, you may have more flexibility in your hunting locations as well, since you could effectively set up in the middle of fields. However, if you plan to use a blind, I recommend setting it up several days or even weeks before your hunt. If the silhouette of the blind is distinguishable, doves that frequently fly over the area where you set it up will need time to become accustomed to it.

Woodcocks

In recent years I have found a new wingshooting favorite in Delaware—woodcocks. Woodcocks, or timberdoodles as they are sometimes called, are frequently overlooked game birds that are pursued by relatively few Delaware hunters. The smallish, quail-size birds provide for challenging shooting and excellent hunting, especially if you hunt them with a good bird dog. Through my experiences hunting woodcocks over the past several years, I have concluded that woodcocks are the last bastion of ground-dwelling game birds in Delaware, especially in the northern two-thirds of the state. Judging by the facts that I have not harvested a limit of wild quail or pheasants in Delaware in years and that I frequently limit out on woodcocks, it is easy to see why woodcock hunting is my favorite form of game bird hunting.

What the Heck is a Woodcock?

Author Steven M. Kendus displaying a woodcock harvested while hunting near saplings in Kent County, Delaware.

I asked a lot of hunters about woodcock hunting and if they had seen any woodcocks while deer or small game hunting. Frequently, my question was answered with, "What the heck is a woodcock?" There you have it. One of the reasons a lot of hunters don't pursue woodcocks is because they have no idea what woodcocks even are! After all, if they don't know what they look like, how can they hunt them?

To an unknowing hunter who is lucky enough to see one, a woodcock resembles any number of small shore- and marsh-dwelling birds that frequent the Delaware coastline, mainly because of their long bills that are used for probing mud, soil, and sand for food. They are about the size of quail, but rounder, and are perfectly colored to blend in with the forest floor. Woodcocks are mostly shades of brown and gray with rust and black accents, and their breasts are a much lighter tan. Their eyes are relatively big and are situated high and back on their heads so that they can see their surroundings while they probe for food.

Because of their superb natural camouflage, woodcocks are content to sit tight when potential predators approach. Although dogs can find woodcocks by scent, it is much more difficult for us. I have literally almost stepped on woodcocks while walking to deer stands and while small game hunting, and I was subsequently scared half to death when the birds flushed right in front of me. They flush quickly in a loud, erratic flutter. In flight, their wings make a whistling sound similar to the sounds of flying doves.

While it is improbable to encounter woodcocks while they are on the ground, it is more common to see them in flight during their spring mating season. Male woodcocks perform an aerobatic "dance" to attract females in which they fly upward making wide spirals. Near the top of their climbs, they vibrate their wings, and then dive down in zigzag fashions landing near a female. I have witnessed this courtship while standing at the firing line of a rifle range of all places! It is truly a peculiar, yet majestic, sight.

Habitat and Food

Although Cape May, New Jersey is considered one of the best woodcock hunting locations in the eastern United States (if not *the* best), Delaware has to be considered next in line. Some woodcocks remain in Delaware year round, but most are migratory. They normally breed in the northern United States and Canada, and most birds migrate to the southern

These Delaware-harvested woodcocks have long bills and big, high-set eyes. They are mostly shades of brown and gray with rust and black accents. Their breasts are a much lighter tan.

states in the winter. One of the major migratory flyways of woodcocks is the Atlantic Seaboard, where woodcocks make many short flights in their treks south. Directly in their flight path is the Delaware Bay, which presents them with a challenge due to the long, nonstop flights needed to cross from New Jersey to Delaware. Because the woodcocks need to rest and feed before embarking on their journey across the Delaware Bay, they frequently assemble in large groups in Cape May. Likewise, the woodcocks need to rest and refuel after they cross the Bay, which puts them right smack in prime Delaware hunting territory.

Woodcocks feed mostly on worms since their flexible bills are specially adapted for probing for and catching worms in soil, sand, mud, and leaf litter. When considering locations for

Although Cape May is considered one of the best woodcock hunting locations in the eastern United States, Delaware has to be considered next in line.

woodcock hunting, consider possible woodcock assembly areas first, and consider spots within those areas that are potentially rich in woodcock food second. In many cases, there is ample food at the assembly locations, so the assembly and feeding spots may be one and the same. Since woodcocks look for worm-rich, unfrozen ground to feed on, focus your woodcock hunts on boggy areas, stream and river edges, flooded fields with some dry areas, and spots of thawed ground caused by underground pipes or springs.

Woodcocks can also be found in high concentrations in areas of new forest growth, where young trees are densely grouped and are no more than 10-15 feet high. The closely

Curt Barkus and Gus with a limit of woodcocks harvested in Kent County, Delaware.

packed, relatively low treetops provide adequate cover for woodcocks, and oftentimes the new growth forest floor is rich in worms due to the moist ground caused by leaf litter and low sunlight.

Delaware Woodcock Hunting Season

Woodcock season in Delaware is usually divided into two segments, one in mid-November through early December, and one that lasts for about a week in late December. The daily bag limit is typically three birds, and legal hunting times are usually 30 minutes before official sunrise to official sunset.[46] Woodcocks can be active at any time of day or night, so time of day is of little concern when hunting them. I have hunted woodcocks just after dawn, in mid-morning, and in the afternoon with good results.

In addition to normal licensing requirements, all Delaware woodcock hunters must register with the Federal Harvest Information Program (H.I.P.) so that the Delaware Division of Fish & Wildlife and the United States Fish and Wildlife Service can develop reliable estimates of the number of woodcock harvested.[47] The estimates enable biologists to make sound decisions concerning hunting seasons, bag limits, and woodcock population management.

Woodcocks are similar in size and flight mechanics to quail, and their brushy habitat resembles quail habitat. The woodcocks' physical similarities to quail, coupled with the fact that woodcock hunts may involve long walks through rough, hilly, and wet terrain, mean that hunters should use fast-shooting, lightweight shotguns for these peculiar birds. I began hunting woodcock with a heavy, semi-automatic 12-gauge, but I soon switched to a 20-gauge with a short barrel that allowed for quicker shouldering, swinging, and shooting through brush and trees. Size 7 ½ or 8 high-velocity loads are optimal.

As with hunting all migratory birds, be sure to check all applicable federal regulations and Delaware hunting laws and regulations as established in the annual *Delaware Hunting & Trapping Guide*.

---

[46] *2010-2011 Delaware Waterfowl Season Summary*
[47] *Delaware Hunting & Trapping Guide*, 34.

Woodcock Hunting Hotspots

As mentioned earlier, woodcocks are pursued by relatively few Delaware hunters. As such, gaining access to private land to hunt woodcocks may not be a monumental task. I would even guess that after asking some land owners for permission to hunt woodcocks on their property, they would respond with the common question, "What the heck is a woodcock?" They may even sneer as they grant you permission, since they think there are no such birds on their property. Check aerial photos and topographic maps, and remember to consider the Atlantic flyway when looking for private land to hunt. After finding some potential hunting spots, knock on some doors or leave notes in mailboxes, if need be. This tactic just may pay off.

If you plan to hunt woodcocks on Delaware public land, many good locations exist. My dog Gus and I frequently hunt woodcocks at Augustine Wildlife Area and Chesapeake and Delaware Canal Wildlife Areas in New Castle County and Blackbird State Forest and Blackiston Wildlife Area in Kent County. I have found that there are usually more woodcocks in these areas in the earlier segment of the season, and I have harvested woodcocks at each location.

Techniques

Watch the Weather

The majority of woodcocks you will encounter in Delaware are only stopping for short periods of time during their southward migration. Through experience, my hunting partners and I have found that weather seems to influence the number of woodcocks we encounter on our hunts. If the weather the night before was windy and/or rainy, we seemingly encountered more birds on the ground during the morning. Our unscientific conclusion is that the woodcocks do not like to fly long distances in foul weather. Therefore, we watch for bad weather during the woodcock season and usually try to hunt on those foul weather days.

Likewise, consider temperature when planning your woodcock hunts. If sub-freezing temperatures have been in place in the area for several days, it is a good bet that many woodcocks have moved on to locales farther south where they have better access to food. However, even if temperatures have been near freezing for an extended period, hunt the banks of running water creeks and streams. The soil just near the water may be a little warmer and may attract hungry woodcocks.

During a December woodcock hunt in Kent County I tried this tactic. My hunting partner Curt, Gus, and I hunted the banks of a stream with a 2-inch thick layer of ice on it. The ground was semi-frozen, and early-morning frost was heavy on the grass and leaves. Within 100 yards of walking along the stream edges, Gus found five woodcocks, of which we harvested three.

Hunt Saplings

When I first began hunting the strange, little woodcock, I mainly focused on boggy areas and streams. I harvested my fair share of birds, but I never really encountered high concentrations of birds in one area. After doing some research and overcoming my doubts, I tried hunting patches of saplings. To my surprise, I encountered more birds — in higher concentrations — than I did when hunting the bogs.

Some of my best woodcock hunts took place in acres full of saplings. While turkey hunting in the spring of 2009, I encountered several areas of recently cleared and replanted forest. I noticed that the saplings were packed closed together and were no more than ten feet high. I made a note to return to these areas during the fall woodcock season. On my first two woodcock hunts at these locations, I limited out within 30 minutes. I was able to drive to the hunting spot, hunt, drive home, and be at work by 8:45 AM. That's a good woodcock hunt.

To find good patches of newly planted trees, stop by the forestry office of any Delaware state forest. Speak with a forester or ranger and ask him or her about newly planted patches. In many cases they will be able to direct you to locations, provide you with maps, and give you feedback regarding game they've seen in those areas.

Return to the Same Spots

Another thing that my hunting partners and I have learned about woodcock hunting is that good rest stops and feeding locations appeal to all woodcocks. The birds must all be searching for the same type of terrain, so if one group of birds finds an optimal location, chances are other groups will, too.

I really love this aspect of woodcock hunting. My hunting partners and I typically stick to the same four or five woodcock hunting locations year after year, and the birds always seem to be near the same spots. This seemingly foolproof method of selecting hunting locations saves a lot of time in scouting, planning, and driving. Granted, sapling patches have grown up in some cases, but even with those, we found woodcocks nearby.

Before searching for new spots to hunt, always consider the old, faithful ones. Keep a journal or blog of your hunts so that you have an accurate record of your hunting locations, bird sightings, and harvest totals.

Crows

Considered "varmint hunting" by many, hunting American crows is a superb way to sharpen your wingshooting skills and to beat the blues brought about by the end of deer season. When I was first asked to go crow hunting by some friends, I laughed and thought it sounded ridiculous. I thought hunting crows would be like shooting fish in a barrel, but I tagged along anyway. After wasting a box of shells and only having a few crows to show for it, I was soon the one being laughed at. Crows are wary, intelligent birds, and their keen eyesight and fondness for high flying make them formidable opponents.

Habitat and Food

As with doves, crows can be found in all parts of Delaware. Crows prefer to nest in tall, sheltered trees near open areas, such as farms, fields, parks and beaches, and they normally live in family groups that establish and defend large home territories. Family groups consist of crows of various ages, from fledglings to fully mature adults, and they can frequently be observed feeding together or swarming (called mobbing) predators, like hawks and owls.

One of the most fascinating aspects of crows is their winter roosting behavior. During the fall and winter months, many crow family groups fly from their normal territories each evening to a communal roost location that draws crows from miles around. The crow roosts, which can host hundreds to tens of thousands of crows each night, provide the crows with sheltered sleeping areas that offer them some protection from predators. The absolute best way to hunt Delaware crows is to find a communal roost location. Once a major roost is establish, the crows usually return to the same location year after year.

Crows are omnivorous, and from what I have seen, they are not picky eaters. Scientifically, a crow's diet consists of worms, insects, fruits, seed, nuts, eggs, and small animals like baby birds, mice, and frogs. However, I have seen crows eating everything from roadkill and fried chicken to cut squid bait and French fries. Crows usually forage for food by walking on the ground and turning over leaves, debris, and garbage in search of tasty morsels, but they will also scavenge animal carcasses and sometimes actively hunt small, easily accessible animals. Crows are resourceful feeders, and they may use gravity, automobiles, and other predators to assist them in procuring food. They may carry hard nuts into the air and drop them to the ground hoping they crack, and they may even drop the nuts directly onto highways so that vehicles can aid in cracking the shells. Likewise, they may wait for buzzards or other animals to penetrate thick animal hides before they begin feeding.

Hunting crows at a wintertime roost can be a superb way to sharpen your wingshooting skills and to beat the blues brought about by the end of deer season.

Delaware Crow Hunting Season

Delaware's crow season is a long one, though most people don't take full advantage of it. While the dates vary from year to year, Delaware crow season is usually open for about nine consecutive months—approximately from the beginning of July through the end of March—with only the typical spring breeding season off-limits. Additionally, Delaware crow hunting is usually only permitted on Thursdays, Fridays, and Saturdays during the open season.[48]

The majority of crow hunters I know reserve their crow hunting time for late winter, when they are trying to beat the post-deer season blues, or early fall, when they are sharpening up for waterfowl and small game hunting. Although crows can be successfully hunted during other times of the year, many hunters are preoccupied with pursuing fish or other game. Hunting hours are 30 minutes before official sunrise to official sunset, and there is typically no bag limit for crows.

Crows are big, strong birds, and their inclination to fly high when threatened means hunters may need some strong firepower to knock them down. I typically hunt crows in February and March in a roost location near the Delaware River where wind is usually a big factor. If the wind will be blowing the crows over me, I opt for a semi-automatic 12-gauge with size 5 or 6, long-range loads. If the wind will be slowing the crows and pushing them downward as they fly in, I may change to a 20-gauge with size 6, long-range loads. Regardless of the type of gun used to hunt crows, do not scrimp on ammo. The pellets of cheap loads seemingly

---

[48] Delaware Department of Natural Resources and Environmental Control, *2010-2011 Delaware Migratory Game Bird Season Summary*.

bounce off crows (if you even reach them), so be sure to use quality shells.

As with hunting all migratory birds, before hunting crows be sure to check all applicable federal regulations and Delaware hunting laws and regulations as established in the annual *Delaware Hunting & Trapping Guide* and associated publications.

Crow Hunting Hotspots

One of the greatest things about crow hunting is that you can create your own hotspots! If you are not lucky enough to find a major crow roost on land where you have permission to hunt, you can use the crow's territorial and defensive nature to lure him in.

When looking for good locations to set up for crow, just watch the skies, treetops, and fields. During your scouting trips or hunts for other game species, notice and log where you see crows. Count the numbers in a group, watch where they land, and observe the directions they fly. Try to discern the patterns, habits, and territories of family groups, and look for good hiding locations where you can set up to hunt the birds. After finding some potential hunting locations near crow family groups, find an easily recognizable tree, stump, fencepost, or some other object where you can set an owl decoy. Set up the owl decoy, add a few crow decoys and some calling, and voilà — you now have a crow hunting hotspot! Any crows within visible range will be drawn toward the owl, and you should be presented with some fine shooting.

An effective crow decoy spread consists of full-body crow decoys and an easily visible owl decoy with lifelike wings.

Techniques

When Crows Attack!

As mentioned above, enticing crows to attack a predator decoy can lead to enjoyable and successful hunts. Crow families will swarm and dive at their natural predators, so incorporating an owl decoy into your hunts is a sure way to draw crows into range. A plastic owl decoy can be purchased for less than twenty dollars from hunting supply, garden, and home supply stores, and it is an effective decoy right out of the box. However, to add realism to an owl decoy, try wiring two real goose or turkey wings together and attaching them to the back of the decoy. The sheen and movement of the feathers will make the plastic decoy look more lifelike. Set the owl decoy in a location that can be easily seen by crows in flight. Place the owl in a leafless tree, on a sand mound, on a log in a field, or in a snow-covered clearing.

To further entice the crows, set up crow decoys on the ground and in some trees near the owl. Inexpensive full-body and silhouette decoys made of foam and/or plastic can be effective, but new, high-quality decoys are optimal. Some new crow decoys use hard plastic, full-body molds covered in black, velvety material (known as flocking), and they look just about identical to the real thing. If you really want to get fancy with your decoy spreads, try placing an animated (wing-flapping) crow decoy at the base of the owl decoy to give the appearance of a struggling crow caught in the owl's talons. If you have harvested a crow and don't have an animated decoy, place the crow at the base of the owl instead.

Another technique that my hunting partners and I use is incorporating a kite-like, flying crow decoy into our spread. We anchor the decoy's string in the ground and allow the wind to hover the decoy about 15 feet over the decoy spread. It works phenomenally.

Call Them In

When attempting to attract the attention of crows, calling is crucial. Crows make a variety of sounds, with most being some variation of the familiar "caw" sound. The "caws" can be short (less than one second) or long (about one to three seconds), and they can be repeated in succession and/or doubled-up to make "caw-caw" sounds. Different calls are used by crows for different purposes, such as alerts, defense, assembly, and locating other groups. The best way to

To add realism to your crow decoy spread, place a harvested crow at the base of your owl decoy and use the dying crow sound when calling.

determine which crow calls are used for which purposes is to listen to crows in the field.

When crow hunting, I use several mouth calls, since they each have a distinct tone and range. Wooden and acrylic crow calls are effective, but I especially like acrylic calls for making the "dying crow" sound. When crows are circling the decoys but none has fully committed to coming within range, I make a long, whining, muffled call that sounds like an injured or dying crow. In many cases, the crows hear this call and they dive bomb (for lack of a better description) the owl decoy. This dying crow call is especially effective if an animated decoy or dead crow is placed near the base of the owl.

Because batteries have much more stamina than my lungs, I also use an automated caller when crow hunting. There are many automated calling systems on the market, but they all consist of a unit that plays recordings, a speaker, a set of controls (usually remote), and a catalog of sounds. When shopping for an automated caller, be aware that many systems only play recording media (tapes, disks, cards) made specifically for that unit. Also, be sure to research the available crow sounds that can be played on a specific unit. When hunting with the automated caller, set the speaker among the decoys, but be sure to camouflage or hide it. Only call periodically, especially when birds are visible. Use high volume when the birds are far away, but lower the volume as the birds approach, so you don't spook the crows. When applicable, use your mouth call along with the automated caller to make the dying crow call.

6

Waterfowl Hunting

Delaware makes up the majority of the Delmarva Peninsula (with portions of Maryland and Virginia completing the land mass) and is directly between the Chesapeake Bay and the Delaware River, Delaware Bay, and Atlantic Ocean. Located within the Atlantic Flyway where millions of ducks and geese annually migrate from their northern breeding grounds to their southern wintering grounds and back, Delaware's plethora of water features and agricultural fields offer waterfowlers a duck and goose hunting paradise.

Volumes can be (and have been) written on waterfowl hunting, comprehensively covering such topics as duck and goose behavior, decoy spread set up, calling, blind building, water versus field hunting, and strategies for different species. Perhaps a subsequent book of this series on Delaware hunting will focus solely on waterfowl hunting, but for now, we will stick to the basics. This chapter offers a basic introduction to Delaware waterfowl hunting and provides information regarding Delaware waterfowl hunting seasons, hotspots, and some techniques that have proven effective in Delaware.

Ducks

Just as thousand of hunters anxiously await and prepare for the annual opening day of deer season, Delaware waterfowlers mark their calendars for the opening day of duck season. Duck hunters can be found in the late summer and early fall cleaning and painting decoys, blinds, and boats; applying reeds and grasses to blinds; training their retrievers; and spending hours at the shooting range practicing their wingshooting. Many Delaware waterfowl hunters also participate in deer and small game hunting, but there are some hunters who hunt waterfowl exclusively. These die-hard waterfowlers know the superb hunting that Delaware has to offer.

Types of Ducks found in Delaware

While Delaware hosts several species of ducks year round, many more show up in Delaware waters and fields during the late summer, fall, and winter migration periods. A big part of duck hunting is the ability to identify different species of ducks (in flight and at rest), so it is important to be aware of the species of ducks that are typically harvested in Delaware. The table on the following page, while not all inclusive, lists duck species that were harvested in Delaware during the 2006-2007 and 2007-2008 hunting seasons and provides estimated harvest totals for each.

2007 and 2008 Delaware Duck Harvest Statistics (Preliminary U.S. Fish and Wildlife Service Estimates)[49]		
Species	2007	2008
Mallard	16,201	22,625
Black Duck	5,849	7,283
Gadwall	2,690	3,884
Wigeon	643	1,165
Green-winged Teal	9,709	11,361
Cinnamon Teal	234	0
Northern Shoveler	936	583
Northern Pintail	1,228	2,428
Wood Duck	5,088	3,496
Redhead	0	97
Canvasback	58	0
Greater Scaup	58	97
Lesser Scaup	117	680
Ring-necked Duck	760	874
Goldeneyes	175	97
Bufflehead	2,398	3,787
Ruddy Duck	58	583
Long-tailed Duck	720	200
Eiders	180	0
Scoters	1,800	1,500
Hooded Mergansers	468	486
Other Mergansers	409	680

Although the above table lists many commonly harvested duck species, hunters occasionally come across others.

---

[49] U.S. Fish and Wildlife Service, 2009. *Migratory Bird Hunting Activity and Harvest During the 2007 and 2008 Hunting Seasons.*

A view from inside a duck blind shows a mallard and two teal.

Domestic mallards, mallard hybrids, goldeneyes, eiders, and other species of ducks may visit Delaware, frequently due to weather events that affect their normal migration flight patterns or their winter food sources. Before shooting at any ducks, be sure you can positively identify them and be sure you are thoroughly familiar with all federal and Delaware regulations related to seasons and bag and possession limits.

Duck Hunting Seasons and Regulations

Delaware establishes its duck hunting seasons, bag limits, and shooting hours in accordance with federal wildlife management guidelines. Delaware typically implements a split season consisting of three segments and may implement separate special seasons. According to the United States Fish and Wildlife Service:

> States have been allowed to divide their hunting period for most species and groups of birds into 2 or sometimes 3 nonconsecutive segments in order to take advantage of species-specific peaks of abundance. Generally, special seasons focus on those species considered to be more lightly utilized than others. Special seasons are usually, but not always, in addition to the regular season.[50]

Traditionally, Delaware's duck hunting season segments include about 10 days from late October to early November, about 10 days from mid-November to the beginning of December, and about 30-40 days from Mid-December to late-January. Additionally, a special early teal season is usually held in September and applies to a limited geographic area

---

[50] U.S. Fish and Wildlife Service: Division of Migratory Bird management. *Regulations.*

comprised of coastal areas south of the Chesapeake and Delaware Canal to Lewes, east of Routes 1, 113/113A, and 1. For all seasons and segments, shooting hours are 30 minutes before official sunrise to until official sunset.[51]

During the regular duck season, daily bag limits are typically six ducks, but harvest numbers for some individual species are regulated. For example, for the 2010-2011 hunting season, the daily limit is six ducks, but individual limits are placed on scaup (2), black ducks (1), mallards (4, with no more than 2 hens), pintails (2), wood ducks (3), redheads (2), canvasbacks (1), scoters (4), and several other species. Keep in mind that separate limits may be imposed for special seasons (teal) and species (mergansers). Also, certain species may be off-limits, like harlequins. The possession limit is typically twice the daily bag limit.[52]

In addition to regular hunting licenses, Delaware duck hunters 16 years of age or older must also purchase and possess a Delaware state waterfowl stamp and a Federal Migratory Bird Hunting Stamp to hunt ducks in Delaware. Additionally, all Delaware duck hunters must register with the Federal Harvest Information Program (H.I.P.) so that the Delaware Division of Fish & Wildlife and the United States Fish and Wildlife Service can develop reliable estimates of the number of ducks harvested.[53] The estimates enable biologists to make sound decisions concerning hunting seasons, bag limits, and duck population management.

By federal mandate, duck hunters must use steel or other approved non-toxic shot when hunting ducks. Because of its toxic effect on waterfowl, lead shot has been banned for

---

[51] 2010-2011 Delaware Waterfowl Season Summary.
[52] 2010-2011 Delaware Waterfowl Season Summary.
[53] 2010-2011 Delaware Waterfowl Season Summary.

Duck hunter Jeff Kirk poses with a wood duck on Thousand Acres Marsh in New Castle County.

waterfowl hunting in the United States since 1991. As listed in the 2010-2011 *Delaware Hunting & Trapping Guide*, federally approved non-toxic shot includes steel, bismuth-tin, tungsten-iron, tungsten-polymer, tungsten-matrix, tungsten-nickel-iron, and tungsten-iron-nickel-tin.

Because of the varying sizes and flight speeds of duck species, it is impossible to pinpoint a perfect type of gun or load for duck hunting. Many skilled duck hunters agree that steel #3 shot has the best all-around performance on ducks, although newer, heavier, non-toxic loads are gaining popularity. With many shotgun models capable of firing 3-inch and 3.5-inch shells, some hunters prefer to use the 3.5" shells to give them extra distance when hammering difficult ducks that will not commit fully to the decoys. I opt for a 12-gauge, semi-automatic shotgun with an improved cylinder choke, though many hunters swear by their old-school, pump-action models because they believe their guns are less likely to foul or freeze during hunting. (Even though I use a semi-automatic shotgun for ducks, I can honestly say that I had the shotgun jam during a waterfowl hunt. My guide just about had birds landing on top of the blind, I squeezed the trigger in an attempt to harvest a bird about 10 yards away, and I got nothing! The gun did not fire, and I went home empty handed.) Whichever gun, choke, and ammo combination you choose to use, I suggest patterning your shots before heading to the marshes or fields. Different shot types will create different patterns at different distances, so be sure to pattern your gun whenever you think about changing loads.

Before hunting ducks in Delaware, check all applicable federal regulations and Delaware regulations, as established in the annual *Delaware Hunting & Trapping Guide* and any supplemental information published by the Delaware Division of Fish & Wildlife.

Duck Hunting Hotspots

Similar to deer and turkey hunting in Delaware, many Delaware hunters will tell you that duck hunting private land is the way to go. With all of the private farm ponds and agricultural fields that draw ducks in during the annual migrations, it is easy to see why some hunters feel this way. However, what some hunters fail to realize is that Delaware's public duck hunting areas are among the best in the country. During their migrations, ducks bound for their southern wintering grounds stop to rest and feed in almost all of Delaware's public hunting locations, but they can be found in great numbers in the fields, ponds, and estuaries of Prime Hook and Bombay Hook National Wildlife Refuges.

Bombay Hook National Wildlife Refuge, located along the Delaware Bay, east of Smyrna in Kent County, is just shy of 16,000 acres, 80% of which is tidal salt marsh. It is mainly a breeding ground and refuge for migrating birds, and is a prized hunting location. As described by the United States Fish and Wildlife Service:

> The refuge has one of the largest expanses of nearly unaltered tidal salt marsh in the mid-Atlantic region. It also includes 1,100 acres of impounded fresh water pools, brushy and timbered swamps, 1,100 acres of agricultural lands, and timbered and grassy upland. The general terrain is flat and less than ten feet above sea level.[54]

Prime Hook National Wildlife Refuge is one of the best existing wetland habitat areas along the Atlantic Coast and is subsequently highly regarded by Delaware duck hunters. Located in Sussex County, north of Lewes and along the Delaware Bay, the refuge consists of 10,000 acres, including 4,200 acres of freshwater marshes that are intensively managed as important stop-over sites for migrating birds. The remainder of the refuge is comprised of salt marshes, grasslands, woodlands, scrub-brush habitats, ponds, a 7-mile long creek, and agricultural fields. According to the United States Fish and Wildlife Service, more than 80,000 ducks can be found at the refuge during peak migration periods.

If you choose to test your hunting luck and skill at Bombay Hook or Prime Hook, be aware that specific, more restrictive hunting regulations may be in effect for national

---

[54] U.S. Fish and Wildlife Service, *Bombay Hook National Wildlife Refuge*.

Sunset on a Bombay Hook National Wildlife Refuge marsh silhouettes ducks on the water.

wildlife refuges. Hunting dates, days of the week, and available areas may differ from the general Delaware duck hunting regulations. Typically, duck blinds are issued via daily lottery (on available hunting days) at checking stations within each area.

Other Delaware public duck hunting hotspots include: Chesapeake and Delaware Canal and Cedar Swamp Wildlife Areas in New Castle County; Woodland Beach and Little Creek Wildlife Areas in Kent County; and Assawoman Wildlife Area in Sussex Counties. Many Delaware public hunting areas have state blinds that are issue through daily lotteries at the checking stations on each area. A $20 permit is required to use waterfowl blinds on State-owned blinds assigned through lotteries. One permit is needed for each hunter in the blind.[55] Check with the Delaware Division of Fish & Wildlife for more information regarding purchasing and using the blind permits.

Techniques

Total Concealment

We talk about using good camouflage when deer and turkey hunting, and we know that camouflage is important when duck hunting. However, many of us fail to consider how important it is to *totally* camouflage or conceal ourselves and our blinds when duck hunting. A lot of us are accustomed to camouflaging and concealing ourselves from onward looking turkeys and deer, but we don't care too much about what's above us. Using this same line of thinking inevitably hurts duck hunters.

When ducks seem to be committing to your decoys and they inexplicable flare off at the last minute, this, in many cases, is because they saw you or your blind. When at the right overhead angle, they saw glistening from your glasses, they saw you grab your gun, they saw a large box sitting where trees were supposed to be — take your pick. To prevent ducks from seeing anything that could potentially spook them, remember to use some sort of overhead concealment. Place pop-up doors or covers on the tops of blinds, and cover them with varying levels of natural looking camouflage materials (like marsh grasses, phragmites, reeds, and branches). If you are not hunting from a blind or you cannot cover your blind, wear camo that matches your surroundings and covers exposed skin. Cover your head, face, and hands,

---

[55] *Delaware Hunting & Trapping Guide*, 43.

and, especially if you wear glasses in the field, do not look up until absolutely necessary. Likewise, use matte-finish, camouflage guns that produce little or no glare; totally conceal your boat; and be sure your dog cannot he seen or heard.

Note: These duck hunting techniques also apply to hunting Canada geese and snow geese.

Add Motion to Your Decoys

It seems that with every duck season the decoys *look* more realistic. In fact, some of the new decoys look so real that hunters have difficulty telling them apart from real ducks. There is only one problem with these realistic-looking decoys — they still don't *act* like real ducks. I am convinced that sooner or later all hunters will upgrade to these modern, super-realistic decoys, and most of us will then sit in our blinds and admire our decoys as the ducks fly by.

To really make your decoy spread appeal to ducks, it is imperative that you add movement. If you have ever looked at ducks on a pond, you know that they do not just sit there. They swim and dive and subsequently create ripples, wakes, and splashes. If you can give your decoy spread the appearance of live, moving ducks, you will draw more ducks in than the majority of the other hunters who are just using stationary rigs. Creating motion in your decoy spread can be as simple as tying a jerk string to the decoys and jerking it periodically, or it can be as complex as using a machine with a remote control that makes your decoys dive, swim, thrash, or bob in the water. Regardless of the complexity, any movement is better than none.

To manually add movement to your spread, string groups of your decoys together and attach a long string to each group that reaches to your blind or hiding spot. When ducks are visible, periodically jerk the string, being careful to conceal your arm's movement. If possible, run the string through an opening in the blind. If you cannot rig a jerk string to your decoys, you can create movement by simply splashing or kicking the water. The waves and ripples created by the splashing will move the ducks, giving them a more realistic appearance.

For automatic motion in your decoy spread, consider purchasing some of the newer, animated decoys that are sold at hunting supply stores. There are animated decoys that swim, flap, fly, dive, and shake, and they can provide the needed movement that will entice ducks to land in your spread.

Note: These duck hunting techniques also apply to hunting Canada geese and snow geese.

Watch the Weather

We've all heard the expression, "perfect weather for a duck," but it may be a bit misleading to duck hunters. Many duck hunters will tell you that the best days to hunt ducks are in driving wind and rain, others prefer just wind, and still others say that bright, blue-bird days can be effective. While each duck hunter has opinions regarding the best weather to actually hunt in, it may be more important to look at the weather that is driving the ducks southward to Delaware.

During their southward migrations, ducks tend to remain in locations along the Atlantic Flyway until food sources have been depleted or have become inaccessible due to ice or snow

Delawarean Curt Barkus after a successful, multi-species duck hunt.

cover. Therefore, it is a good tactic for duck hunters to monitor the weather in areas farther north in the Flyway. If relatively calm, warm weather is followed by snow, ice, and sub-freezing temperatures in New England, for example, the quick weather change may drive ducks farther south in search of food and open water. Duck hunting in Delaware on days following such weather changes can be extremely effective.

Additionally, when Delaware waters begin to freeze up, look for sources of open water. Consider hunting bigger bodies of moving water, like the Delaware River, and some of the smaller, flowing creeks and streams that ultimately lead to the River. Delaware duck hunters who find open waters during major freeze-ups are frequently rewarded with good harvests.

Note: These duck hunting techniques also apply to hunting Canada geese and snow geese.

Canada Geese

Because of its location in the Atlantic Flyway, the area between the Chesapeake Bay and the Delaware Bay is considered one of the best goose hunting locations in the United States. With the multitude of agricultural fields and bodies of water essentially acting as goose magnets, waterfowl hunters from across America travel to this region to hunt Canada geese and snow geese. The table on the following page illustrates goose hunting's popularity in Delaware.

2007 and 2008 Delaware Goose Harvest Statistics (Preliminary U.S. Fish and Wildlife Service Estimates)[56]		
Species	2007	2008
Canada Goose	21,996	28,637
Snow Goose	7,911	14,318

About Canada Geese

Canada geese are one the best known waterfowl species in North America. They are found in just about all parts of Canada and the United States, though their ranges differ depending upon the time of year. Most Canada geese breed in the extreme northern United States and Canada and migrate to winter feeding grounds in the southern half of the United States. However, many Canada geese establish year-round residency in the northern half of the U.S., including the Mid-Atlantic region, and are considered a nuisance species by some. Their voracious appetites and droppings can lead to diminished crop harvests and polluted ponds, yards, golf courses, and even city parks.

Canada geese spend most of their time on water, but they nest and usually feed on land. They eat plant matter exclusively and are fond of grasses, grains, sedges, and berries. Canada geese migrate south in the winter to find food, which leads tens of thousands of geese directly to Delaware.

---

[56] U.S. Fish and Wildlife Service, 2009. *Migratory Bird Hunting Activity and Harvest During the 2007 and 2008 Hunting Seasons.*

Canada goose hunting is a strong tradition. This photo from 1971 shows Matt Mille with a goose harvested among silhouette decoys.

Canada Goose Hunting Seasons and Regulations

In accordance with federal wildlife management guidelines, Delaware typically implements a split goose season consisting of three segments. The first segment, a resident Canada goose season, lasts for about two weeks from early- to mid-September. This resident Canada goose season is aimed at controlling the population of Canada geese that remain in Delaware year round. The daily bag limit for resident Canada geese is generous, with limits in the 10-15 birds range. The migratory Canada goose season typically consists of two segments, one segment usually from mid-November to the beginning of December and one segment from mid-December to late-January. The daily bag limit for migratory birds is usually in the 1-2 birds range, with the possession limit usually set at twice the daily bag limit. Legal shooting hours are typically 30 minutes before official sunrise to official sunset for migratory geese, but regulations may change year to year.[57]

In addition to regular hunting licenses, Delaware hunters 16 years of age or older must also purchase and possess a Delaware state waterfowl stamp and a Federal Migratory Bird Hunting Stamp to hunt Canada geese in Delaware. Additionally, all Delaware Canada goose hunters must register with the Federal Harvest Information Program (H.I.P.) so that the Delaware Division of Fish & Wildlife and the United States Fish and Wildlife Service can develop reliable estimates of the number of geese harvested.[58] The estimates enable biologists to make sound decisions concerning hunting seasons, bag limits, and goose population management.

By federal mandate, Canada goose hunters must use approved non-toxic shot when hunting Canada geese. Because of its toxic effect on waterfowl, lead shot has been banned for waterfowl hunting in the United States since 1991. As listed in the 2010-2011 *Delaware Hunting & Trapping Guide*, federally approved non-toxic shot includes steel, bismuth-tin, tungsten-iron, tungsten-polymer, tungsten-matrix, tungsten-nickel-iron, and tungsten-iron-nickel-tin.

---

[57] 2010-2011 Delaware Migratory Game Bird Season Summary.
[58] *Delaware Hunting & Trapping Guide*, 34.

Delaware goose hunter John Antonio frequently hunts Canada geese in Delaware's public and private fields, ponds, lakes, impoundments, streams, and rivers.

Canada geese are big birds, with some weighing more than 15 pounds. Their tough feathers, coupled with their relatively large vital organs, dictate that large shot be used when hunting them. Steel BBB shot is argued to be most effective on Canada geese, but as with hunting ducks, other non-toxic loads and shot sizes are gaining popularity. Twelve-gauge shotguns with modified chokes are the norm, though many hunters prefer the added power and distance of 10-gauge models and shotguns capable of shooting 3.5-inch magnum shells.

Before hunting Canada geese in Delaware, check all applicable federal and Delaware waterfowl hunting regulations. Delaware regulations are printed in the annual

Delaware Hunting & Trapping Guide and other supplemental information published by the Delaware Division of Fish & Wildlife.

Canada Goose Hunting Hotspots

Canada geese can be found all over Delaware and are frequently hunted in public and private fields, ponds, lakes, impoundments, streams, and rivers throughout the state. While Bombay Hook and Prime Hook National Wildlife Refuges are traditional public hotspots for Canada geese, other hot public areas that offer blinds include: Augustine, Chesapeake and Delaware Canal, and Cedar Swamp Wildlife Areas in New Castle County; Woodland Beach and Little Creek Wildlife Areas in Kent County; and Assawoman and Nanticoke Wildlife Areas in Sussex County. In most cases the blinds are issued through daily lotteries at the checking stations on each area. A $20 permit is required to use waterfowl blinds on State-owned blinds assigned through lotteries. One permit is needed for each hunter in the blind.[59] Check with the Delaware Division of Fish & Wildlife for more information regarding purchasing and using the blind permits.

Techniques

Since many duck hunting techniques also apply to Canada geese, be sure to read the *Duck Hunting* section of this chapter for additional tips and techniques to help you harvest Canada geese.

---

[59] *Delaware Hunting & Trapping Guide*, 43.

Scout – Go Where the Geese Have Been

As with most hunting, scouting is effective when pursuing Canada geese. During their migrations, Canada geese usually feed twice a day (once in the morning and once in the afternoon) to build up fat for warmth and to store energy for long flights. After flocks of geese locate a prime feeding location (usually an agricultural or grassy field), they will usually return to the same spot until the food supply is depleted or until they are chased off.

To find prime Canada goose hunting fields, take a drive or walk around any locations you have permission to hunt. Watch for geese already feeding, and watch for more geese landing. If you can pinpoint the fields in which the geese are currently feeding, you can bet that the geese will feed in the same location the following day. Arrive before dawn the following day, giving yourself enough time to set up your decoys and prepare any blinds. If the pattern holds true, your geese will start arriving to feed within the first hours of daylight.

Note: These Canada goose hunting techniques also apply to hunting snow geese.

Sound Like 'Geese'

As someone who thinks it is easier to hand-pick the feathers from a goose than to effectively blow a goose call, I have all the respect in the world for a hunter who can blow a call like Jimi Hendrix played guitar.

John Massey, owner of Shooters Supply in New Castle, Delaware and a former goose calling champion, is one of a select few hunters who can effectively call in geese from just

In order to entice flocks of geese to land in your decoy spread, it is important to sound like multiple calling geese, not just one.

about any distance in just about any weather conditions. Massey, who also worked as a Delaware waterfowl hunting guide in the 1980s and 1990s, has given me 20 years of pointers, but I still sound like a single dying goose when attempting to blow a goose call. The argument can be made that any calling is better than no calling when you are hunting over Canada goose decoys, but it my case, I always question if "bad calling" is better than no calling at all!

If you do not have the opportunity to hunt geese with champion callers, then it is absolutely crucial that you practice calling well before you head out to the hunting blind. Having shared a house with Massey in college, I can attest that he blew that call incessantly—at all times of the day and during all times of the year. After many sleepless hours and my fair share of earplugs, I asked him why he practiced so much. I told him that he already sounded like any goose I ever heard. He responded with, "Anybody can sound like *one* goose. The key is sounding like *an entire flock.*"

When calling Canada geese, remember that you may have anywhere from a few to a few hundred decoys in your spread. In order to entice flocks of geese to land in your decoy spread, it is important to sound like multiple calling geese, not just one. As mentioned at the beginning of this chapter, entire books can be written on effectively calling geese. Because the topic of calling geese is so broad (let alone tough to address without audio), we will not discuss specifics. However, like every other type of hunting, do your research before heading to the field. Listen to live geese in flight, on the ground, and on water. Listen to how their calls change when feeding, when birds on the ground are calling to birds in flight, and when flying birds are looking to land. Study audio and video tapes; try different styles of calls; and practice—a lot. For additional advice and assistance, contact your local hunting supply store to see if they can recommend a goose calling tutor, or look for tutors on the Internet.

> Note: These Canada goose hunting techniques also apply to hunting snow geese.

Snow Geese

About Snow Geese

Snow geese are usually somewhat smaller than Canada geese and are usually mostly white with black wing tips and bill edges. Some snow geese exhibit a blue form (commonly called blue geese), which is dictated by a specific gene. Blue geese heads are usually white, while the remainder of their plumage is shades of gray, possibly with some patches of white.

Snow geese breed in the Arctic region and migrate south in the winter, frequently spending entire winters along the Atlantic coast where food is more plentiful. In fact, one of the largest concentrations of wintering snow geese can be found at Delaware's Bombay Hook National Wildlife Refuge. Migrating snow goose flocks can be immense, sometimes consisting of thousands of birds. Unlike Canada geese that may make wide circles when landing, snow geese drop from the sky in closely packed, tornado-like spirals. When large flocks land, the visibility of their white feathers can be seen by other birds in flight and will usually attract other flocks. Snow geese are herbivorous, eating aquatic plants, grasses, sedges, and grains.

Because relatively few hunters actively pursue snow geese, their populations have been growing exponentially. In some areas, large snow goose populations are destroying nesting habitat and agricultural crops, so hunting seasons and bag limits have been generously increased.

Snow Goose Hunting Seasons and Regulations

In accordance with federal wildlife management guidelines, Delaware has previously implemented split, statewide snow goose seasons consisting of three segments. The first statewide segment usually ran from mid-October to early November, the second segment from late-November to the late-January, and the third segment from late January to early-March. In more recent years, Delaware snow goose

Relatively few hunters actively pursue snow geese, so winter snow goose numbers are high in Delaware.

seasons consisted of a main season running from October through January and a special federally initiated Snow Goose Conservation Order season running from February through mid-April. Any of the segments may have specific rules that regulate days of the week on which hunting is allowed, so be sure you are familiar with the federal and Delaware guidelines.

The national wildlife refuges in Delaware may implement their own snow goose seasons and segments. For example, in 2010-2011, hunting was only allowed on Mondays, Wednesdays, and Fridays at Bombay Hook National Wildlife Refuge with the authorization of a refuge manager.[60]

---

[60] 2010-2011 Delaware Migratory Game Bird Season Summary.

The daily bag limit for snow geese has ranged from 10-25 birds in recent years, while the number of snow geese a hunter can possess is usually unlimited. During the Snow Goose Conservation Order season, bag and possession limits may differ. In 2011, for example, there were no bag or possession limits during the Snow Goose Conservation Order season.

Legal shooting hours are typically 30 minutes before official sunrise to official sunset, although shooting hours are sometimes extended during the Snow Goose Conservation Order season.[61]

In addition to regular hunting licenses, Delaware hunters 16 years of age or older must also purchase and possess a Delaware state waterfowl stamp and a Federal Migratory Bird Hunting Stamp to hunt snow geese in Delaware. Likewise, all Delaware snow goose hunters must register with the Federal Harvest Information Program (H.I.P.) so that the Delaware Division of Fish & Wildlife and the United States Fish and Wildlife Service can develop reliable estimates of the number of geese harvested.[62] The estimates enable biologists to make sound decisions concerning hunting seasons, bag limits, and snow goose population management. For hunters who wish to participate in the Snow Goose Conservation Order season, they must also register for a free conservation order permit.

It is also interesting to note that Delaware and Maryland traditionally have a reciprocal agreement for hunting snow geese. According to the 2010-2011 *Delaware Hunting & Trapping Guide*:

---

[61] 2010-2011 Delaware Migratory Game Bird Season Summary.
[62] *Delaware Hunting & Trapping Guide*, 34.

Delaware hunters can hunt snow geese in Maryland with their Delaware hunting license provided they have a Maryland duck stamp, a Federal Duck Stamp, a Maryland H.I.P. number and are in compliance with Maryland Hunter Safety laws. Maryland hunters can hunt snow geese in Delaware with their Maryland hunting license provided they have a Delaware duck stamp, a Federal Duck Stamp, a Delaware H.I.P. number and are in compliance with the Delaware Hunter Safety laws.[63]

Hunters must use approved non-toxic shot when hunting snow geese. As listed in the 2010-2011 *Delaware Hunting & Trapping Guide*, federally approved non-toxic shot includes steel, bismuth-tin, tungsten-iron, tungsten-polymer, tungsten-matrix, tungsten-nickel-iron, and tungsten-iron-nickel-tin. For gun and ammunition recommendations, please refer to the Canada goose section above.

Before hunting snow geese in Delaware, check all applicable federal and Delaware waterfowl hunting regulations. Delaware regulations are printed in the annual *Delaware Hunting & Trapping Guide* and other supplemental information published by the Delaware Division of Fish & Wildlife.

Snow Goose Hunting Hotspots

As mentioned several times in this chapter, Bombay Hook National Wildlife Refuge is one of the best places in the country to hunt snow geese. Bombay Hook's fields and salt marshes provide superb wintering grounds for snow geese, and as such, hundreds of thousands of snow geese flock to Bombay Hook each year. Bombay Hook National Wildlife

---

[63] *Delaware Hunting & Trapping Guide*, 37.

Chris Antonio, John Antonio, and Russell Marsh with a nice harvest of snow geese in Sussex County, Delaware.

Refuge is located along the Delaware Bay, east of Smyrna in Kent County, and is just shy of 16,000 acres. Specific rules exist for hunting Bombay Hook, so make yourself aware of any snow goose-related regulations prior to hunting at the refuge. Hunting dates, days of the week, and available areas may differ from the general Delaware hunting regulations. Typically, snow goose hunting permits are issued on a first-come, first-served basis until 3:00 p.m. When hunting snow geese at Bombay Hook, a motor boat is necessary to reach the designated hunting areas. No government blinds are provided, and any blinds used must be temporary and removed at the conclusion of the day's hunt.[64]

---

[64] U.S. Fish and Wildlife Service, *Bombay Hook National Wildlife Refuge: Public Waterfowl Hunting Information.*

If you have the ability to hunt snow geese on Delaware private agricultural fields, the approach to finding a good location is inexact. If you happen to see a field full of snow geese, return to the field before dawn the following day. In many cases, the snow geese will return to the same field. If you cannot locate a field where snow geese frequent, it is possible to draw them in with decoys. However, keep in mind that snow geese are used to seeing *thousands* of their brethren together, so you may have to set out *thousands* (or at least hundreds) of decoys to entice them. White, rag-style decoys are typically used for this approach, and they may be more effective when the wind causes the rags to blow. This little bit of added movement may be enough to convince wary birds to land in your decoy spread.

Techniques

Concealment – White Works

We have discussed camouflage and concealment throughout this chapter, but it is important to add some additional information related specifically to snow goose hunting. In many case, snow goose hunters who set up in fields need nothing more than white suits, hats, and gloves to provide them with adequate camouflage. Assuming the hunters set out the hundreds of snow goose decoys needed to draw in the huge flocks of birds, they can easily sit on the ground among the decoys and virtually disappear.

A hunter in a white suit surrounded by hundreds of white decoys can remain undetected by the landing snow geese. To add some additional concealment from the thousands of overheard eyes, some hunters use snow goose decoys, flags, or kits that can be placed on stakes and placed above their heads, or they cover up with white fabric.

Sound Like A Lot of Geese

As previously discussed in the *Canada Geese* section of this chapter, it is important to sound like a flock of Canada geese when hunting them. The same theory holds true for snow geese, except that hunters have to sound like a whole lot more geese!

Any hunter who has been near a huge flock of snow geese will tell you that the sound is almost deafening. The only possible way to sound remotely like a flock of snow geese that is one thousand birds strong is to have multiple hunting partners – each of whom knows how to effectively call snow geese – blow a snow goose call and hope for the best.

It is by no means easy to sound like a huge flock of snow geese while blowing calls. There is a solution, however. During the recently implemented Snow Goose Conservation Orders seasons, hunters are allowed to use electronic calls to harvest snow geese. With pre-recorded snow goose calls readily available for most types of automatic callers, it is a superb idea to use modern technology to help you achieve snow goose hunting success.

Note: Use of electronic calls for snow goose hunting may only be permitted during Snow Goose Conservation Order seasons any are typically prohibited during regular snow goose seasons. Be sure to abide by all regulations in the annual *Delaware Hunting & Trapping Guide* and other supplemental information published by the Delaware Division of Fish & Wildlife.

7

Preserving the Tradition

As hunters, we are distinctly aware that our numbers are dwindling. In Delaware alone, hunting license sales have declined by nearly 30% since 1982[65], and the number of licensed hunters in the United States is following a similar trend. The National Shooting Sports Foundation (NSSF) estimates that there are more than 20 million active hunters in the United States, but what's troubling is that the number of inactive hunters is estimated to be near 23 million[66]. With interest in hunting seemingly fading, it is up to us to preserve the tradition.

Like it or not, we have to shoulder the responsibility of defending our sport to the closed-minded individuals and groups who want to lump us in with drug-dealing thugs who illegally obtain guns, big-game poachers who kill endangered rhinos for their horns, and professional athletes who run dog fighting and gambling operations. As ridiculous as it may

---

[65] Delaware Division of Fish and Wildlife. *Delaware Hunting & Fishing License Statistics.*

[66] National Shooting Sports Foundation, Inc.. *Frequently Asked Questions: How Many Hunters are there in the U.S..?*

*Preserve the hunting tradition by taking a kid – boy or girl –
hunting.*

sound, it is all true. We, as individuals who are dedicated to
preserving our sport, must do everything we can to prove
that we are not deserving of such stereotypes.

While hunting, it is imperative that we abide by all applicable hunting laws and regulations, and that we respect our natural environment. We must continue to purchase hunting licenses, join conservation groups, renew our NRA memberships, and actually volunteer our time to help clean, preserve, and protect the areas that support the wildlife we pursue.

Likewise, we should go out of our way to respect the feelings of non-hunters, for they all hold voting power that could ultimately affect the future of hunting. While we do not have to agree with a word any of them says, it is best to politely avoid confrontations. We have all heard the fur, meat, and gun arguments before, so we will miss nothing by walking away.

Above all, it is absolutely crucial that we share our sport. Any chance you get, take a kid — boy or girl — hunting. Even before that, take a kid to a hunting safety class. Take a kid to the shooting range. Give a kid instruction about proper gun safety and hunting principles. Enroll a kid in an archery program. Buy a kid a coonskin cap. Bring a kid on scouting walks through the woods. The list is endless, but it is up to us to pass on the tradition of hunting. If we stick together, educate our opponents, and share our sport, we will ensure the legacy of our hunting tradition.

References

References

2006-2007 *Delaware Hunting & Trapping Guide* (Delaware Division of Fish & Wildlife, 2006).

2007-2008 *Delaware Hunting & Trapping Guide* (Delaware Division of Fish & Wildlife, 2007).

2010-2011 *Delaware Hunting & Trapping Guide* (Delaware Division of Fish & Wildlife, 2010).

Animals.nationalgeographic.com. *Red Fox.* Retrieved October 16, 2010 from http://animals.nationalgeographic.com/animals/mammals/red-fox.html

Bobwhite Basics. Retrieved August 18, 2007, from http://www.geocities.com/Yosemite/Forest/3030/basics.htm.

Delaware Division of Fish and Wildlife, *2010-2011 Delaware Migratory Game Bird Season Summary.* Retrieved October 3, 2010 from http://www.fw.delaware.gov/Hunting/Documents/2010-2011%20Waterfowl%20Season%20Summary%20Sheet%2008172010%20final.pdf.

Delaware Division of Fish and Wildlife. *Canada Goose Management in Delaware.* (8/2001.) Retrieved June 2, 2007, from http://www.dnrec.state.de.us/fw/canadagoosereport.pdf

Delaware Division of Fish and Wildlife. *Advisory Council On Wildlife & Freshwater Fish Meeting Minutes, May 29, 2007.* Retrieved July 3, 2007, from http://www.dnrec.state.de.us/fw/advisory/acmay01.pdf.

Delaware Division of Fish and Wildlife. *Delaware Hunting & Fishing License Statistics.* Retrieved June 12, 2010 from http://www.fw.delaware.gov/Info/Pages/LicenseStats.aspx.

Delaware Division of Fish and Wildlife. *Peek-A-Boo I See Turkeys; 4,000 Wild Turkeys since 1986, A Restoration Success Story.* Retrieved July 3, 2007, from http://www.fw.delaware.gov/fw/newsStory.asp?offset=250&PRID=1102.

References

Delaware Division of Fish and Wildlife. *2006/07 Delaware White-tailed Deer Harvest Summary*. Retrieved June 12, 2010, from http://www.fw.delaware.gov/NR/rdonlyres/FB634C39-1E14-4090-9779-CD9E0B179D82/0/FW200607DelawareWhitetailedDeerHarvestSummary.pdf.

Delaware Division of Fish and Wildlife. *2007/08 and 2008/09 Delaware White-tailed Deer Harvest Comparison*. Retrieved September 29, 2010, from http://www.fw.delaware.gov/Hunting/Documents/2007-08%20vs.%202008-09%20Harvest%20Comparison%2005222009.pdf

Delaware Division of Fish and Wildlife. *Delaware White-tailed Deer Population within Each of the 17 Deer Management Zones*. Retrieved June 2, 2007, from http://www.fw.delaware.gov/Hunting/Documents/2008-09 Delaware White-tailed Deer Harvest Summary.pdf.

D. Clay Sisson and H. Lee Stribling, *Patterns of Bobwhite Covey Activity*, Albany Area Quail Management Project, Spring 1999.

Dorcas Coleman and Glenn Therres, *Delmarva Fox Squirrel: Shore Lore & Legacy*. Retrieved August 30, 2007 from http://www.dnr.state.md.us/wildlife/nhpdelfox.html.

eNature.com. *Red Fox*. Retrieved October 16, 2010 from http://www.enature.com/flashcard/show_flash_card.asp?recordnumber=ma0021

Fred Ward, Rick Chastain, Eddie Linebarger, David Long, Kenny Vernon, Rick Fowler, Brian Infield, and Randy Guthrie, *Strategic Quail Management Plan* (Arkansas Game and Fish Commission, 2001), 9.

Information Please Database, Pearson Education, Inc. "Delaware" Retrieved August 29, 2007, from http://www.infoplease.com/ipa/A0108194.html.

Joe Rogerson, *Delaware Deer Management Plan 2010 – 2019 A Guide to How and Why Deer are Managed in The First State* (Delaware Department of Natural Resources & Environmental Control Division of Fish & Wildlife, 2010).

Matthew DiBona, *Project Statement, Delaware – Grant W38R-10, Wildlife Investigations – Wild Turkey*. Retrieved October 1, 2010 from http://www.fw.delaware.gov/Hunting/Documents/W38R%20Report%20-%20Turkey%202009%20%28with%20cover%29.pdf.

National Shooting Sports Foundation, Inc.. *Frequently Asked Questions: How Many Hunters are there in the U.S..?* Retrieved August 29, 2007, from http://www.nssf.org/IndustryResearch/FAQ-ans.cfm?Qno=02&AoI=generic.

Quality Deer Management Association. *What is Quality Deer Management?* Retrieved June 10, 2007, from http://www.qdma.com/qdm/.

University of Michigan Museum of Zoology Animal Diversity Web. *Sciurus carolinensis - eastern gray squirrel.* Retrieved August 10, 2007, from http://animaldiversity.ummz.umich.edu/site/accounts/information/Sciurus_carolinensis.html.

U.S. Census Bureau, Population Finder - Delaware. Retrieved September 29, 2010 from http://factfinder.census.gov.

U.S. Fish and Wildlife Service. 2009. *Migratory Bird Hunting Activity and Harvest During the 2007 and 2008 Hunting Seasons.* U.S. Department of the Interior, Washington, D.C. U.S.A.

U.S. Fish and Wildlife Service, *Bombay Hook National Wildlife Refuge.* Retrieved August 26, 2007 from http://www.fws.gov/northeast/bombayhook/.

U.S. Fish and Wildlife Service, *Bombay Hook National Wildlife Refuge: Public Waterfowl Hunting Information.* Retrieved October 10, 2010 from http://www.fws.gov/northeast/bombayhook/bhwaterfowl-brochure.htm.

U.S. Fish and Wildlife Service: Division of Migratory Bird management. *Regulations.* Retrieved August 26, 2007 from http://www.fws.gov/migratorybirds/mgmt/regs.html.

Wikipedia. *Coyote.* Retrieved October 24, 2010 from http://en.wikipedia.org/wiki/Coyote.

Wikipedia. *Mourning Dove.* Retrieved August 29, 2007 from http://en.wikipedia.org/wiki/Mourning_Dove.

About The Author

 Steven M. Kendus is a lifelong Delaware resident and avid outdoorsman dedicated to preserving hunting opportunities, lands, and traditions. He is a professional author, columnist, technical writer, and marketer, and has had various books and articles published. He is an active member of multiple hunting, shooting, and conservation organizations, including the National Rifle Association, National Wild Turkey Federation, Ducks Unlimited, Safari Club International, Brandywine Hundred Rod and Gun Club, and Delaware State Sportmen's Association.

Mr. Kendus is frequently consulted as an authority on Delaware hunting. He has been a speaker at hunting-related community events, a guest on Sirius XM Patriot's Cam & Company, and a guest host for Versus, where he interviewed hunting legends Tred Barta and David Morris.

Mr. Kendus volunteers his marketing and public relations services to Exceptional Care for Children, a state-of-the-art residential healthcare facility located in Newark, Delaware that serves technology-dependent children and their families.

He has a Bachelor of Arts in English – Business and Technical Writing from the University of Delaware and is a senior member of the Society for Technical Communication.

Want More Hunting the First State?

Don't let this be the end of your quest for all things related to *Hunting the First State*! Be sure to check out Hunting The First State and Steven M. Kendus online. Use the tools listed below to participate in interactive discussions, learn new tips and tricks, upload your photos and videos, and follow Kendus on his hunts.

- **Web:** www.HuntingTheFirstState.com

- **Facebook (Group):** Hunting The First State

- **Facebook (Author):** www.facebook.com/ steven.m.kendus

- **Twitter:** www.twitter.com/skendus

- **YouTube:** www.youtube.com/skendus

- **Linked In:** www.linkedin.com/in/skendus

- **PodCasts:** http://itunes.apple.com/us/podcast/ hunting-the-first-state-the/id303484471

- **Newspaper Column:** *The News Journal* / www.DelawareOnline.com

To contact Steven M. Kendus for product field tests and reviews, guest appearances, and speaking engagements, email him at:

- skendus@HuntingTheFirstState.com